ON YOUR
MARK,
GET SET,
GOAL

MEASURING YOUR SUCCESS

Tova Davis, Ed.D.

ON YOUR MARK, GET SET, GOAL
MEASURING YOUR SUCCESS

iUniverse books may be ordered through booksellers or by contacting:

iUniverse
1663 Liberty Drive
Bloomington, IN 47403
www.iuniverse.com
844-349-9409

Because of the dynamic nature of the Internet, any web addresses or links contained in this book may have changed since publication and may no longer be valid. The views expressed in this work are solely those of the author and do not necessarily reflect the views of the publisher, and the publisher hereby disclaims any responsibility for them.

Any people depicted in stock imagery provided by Getty Images are models, and such images are being used for illustrative purposes only. Certain stock imagery © Getty Images.

ISBN: 978-1-6632-3493-3 (sc)
ISBN: 978-1-6632-4253-2 (e)

Library of Congress Control Number: 2022913134

Print information available on the last page.

iUniverse rev. date: 12/08/2022

CONTENTS

INTRODUCTION

I don't have to tell you teaching is tough.

Sure, you might hear snarky remarks from uninformed individuals who mistakenly believe you get your summers off or who view teaching as glorified babysitting. But you know as well as I that an educator is in beast mode from the moment the bell rings. Unlike with many of your friends' workdays, there are no hour-long lunches (let alone bathroom breaks) or opportunities to surf the internet to kill time. Your evenings are not spent binge-watching shows but, rather, grading papers, coaching, or chaperoning events. And those summers you supposedly get off? I'm sure plenty of you have taught summer school or taken classes for continuing education.

More importantly, the work you do in the classroom directly impacts the lives of thousands of future members of society and leaders of our communities—so much so that a great teacher can set a student on a path to realizing her or his full potential, and a not-so-great teacher can prevent a student from finding his or her true calling in life.

By virtue of the fact that you are reading this book, my assumption is that you are either a skilled, effective, and passionate educator who strives for personal growth and enhanced success on the part of your students or a thriving new teacher ready to create a culture of success for your students.

With *On Your Mark, Get Set, Goal*, my hope is that you can combine my experiences, research, and best practices with your own reflections in a manner that helps you achieve your personal and professional best.

Tova Davis, Ed.D.

OVERVIEW

Education isn't rocket science. Well, technically, it can be if you happen to teach physics or advanced mathematics. That said, the actual nuts and bolts of instruction don't need to be complicated to be effective.

As with anything else, if you break up the complex, overarching methods and principles of teaching into smaller pieces you can examine and improve upon, becoming a better educator can be quite easy.

To that end, this book will do four things:

1. establish five primary areas of professional improvement;
2. break these areas into smaller components on which to focus your attention;
3. establish a means for self-reflection and evaluation of your skills and processes; and
4. provide a road map to help you get where you need to be.

GOALS AND OBJECTIVES

On Your Mark, Get Set, Goal is designed to help put you on a path to achieve the following:

- Develop short- and long-terms goals for professional performance and student growth.
  - o No meaningful improvement is going to happen overnight. As with most things, becoming a more effective instructor will entail learning new skills, breaking old habits, and forming new ones. By making small improvements in the short term

and committing to them for the long term, over time, the improvements will be significant and permanent.

- Build self-efficacy for teaching.
  - o Self-efficacy, quite simply, is believing in yourself. Just like a musician, actor, or public speaker, as a teacher, if you don't believe in your message, your audience (in this case, the students) won't buy into it either. Fortunately, with the improvement of your skills comes confidence that will translate into better engagement and shared commitment with your students.
- Communicate self-awareness and purpose about teaching and student performance.
  - o For you to truly teach at your best, it is crucial to be aware of your goals, your outcomes, and your purpose for teaching. Ask yourself why you decided to go into this profession in the first place. Was it to make a difference? Was it simply because you needed a job? Do you genuinely care about the people you serve? What do you really believe about teaching and learning? Reflecting on questions like these can provide self-awareness and help you become a more effective instructor.
- Develop a deeper understanding of teaching standards.
  - o Let's say, for example, you are an Olympic figure skater. Do you think you would have a better chance at winning a medal if you understood what the judges were looking for and the criteria with which you were being scored? Of course you would. In the same vein, your ability to understand the learning targets will improve dramatically with a better grasp of the standards you are working to meet.
- Create personal growth goals.
  - o Not all goals have to be professional. Many of the strategies found in this book are designed to help you achieve more fulfillment in your nonworking life. As we all know, the happier and better adjusted you are in life, the more effective you will be in your job.

DOMAINS FOR REFLECTION

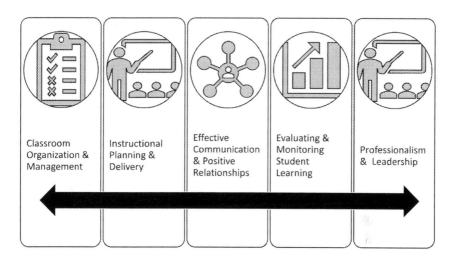

| Classroom Organization & Management | Instructional Planning & Delivery | Effective Communication & Positive Relationships | Evaluating & Monitoring Student Learning | Professionalism & Leadership |

This book will focus on five areas I like to call "domains for reflection." These domains are as follows.

- **Classroom Organization and Management**
  - o Imagine an Amazon distribution center that is not organized. What if the boxes and packing tape weren't in their proper places? What if the inventory was randomly stacked on shelves? What if there weren't systems implemented to optimize workflow? Just like a busy warehouse or factory, a classroom needs to be properly organized and managed to keep lessons running smoothly.
- **Instructional Planning and Delivery**
  - o Success does not happen by coincidence. Rarely does one win a championship or build a successful business by winging it. Similarly, the most effective instruction is the result of well-laid plans that take into account all facets of the educational process, with a heavy focus on the students' needs.
- **Effective Communication and Positive Relationships**
  - o The lynchpin of teaching success is effective communication. This encompasses not only words, but also the media through which the words are delivered; when and how often the messages

are given; and even body language, style of delivery, and other subtleties. Gaining an understanding of these parameters can greatly impact learning. Effective communication can create success in any scenario.

- **Evaluating and Monitoring Student Learning**
  - o Retailers rely heavily on data to target consumers. Corporations utilize metrics, milestones, and sophisticated analytics to gauge and manage their growth. How many times have you driven by a store and then gotten an email or notification from that store? The stores have systems and algorithms that provide data to increase sales and production. As an educator, you can leverage data, metrics, and other tools to teach more effectively.
- **Professionalism and Leadership**
  - o Appearance, preparation, attire, timeliness, communication, and the manner in which you operate can greatly impact the image you convey to parents, colleagues, and, most importantly, students. As such, conveying an image of professionalism can significantly enhance the quality of your teaching.

RATING SCALES

The foundation of this book is self-reflection, and from that, deriving an honest assessment of your abilities in a particular area. To assist in this process, we will use the rating scale outlined below. Specifically, as we work through each skill or technique, you will assign yourself a rating from the following list. Based on these ratings, you can identify areas for improvement.

Developing	I am aware, but I really don't utilize these techniques like I should and I need additional support.
Competent	I am aware, and I occasionally utilize these techniques, however, I am not consistent with implementing these techniques. I may need additional support.
Proficient	I am very skilled in this area, and I utilize these techniques in the classroom with some positive outcomes with students.
Exemplary	I am an expert in this area, and I consistently utilize these techniques in the classroom with significant student results.

- **Developing**
  - o I am aware, but I don't utilize these techniques as I should. I need additional support.
- **Competent**
  - o I am aware, and I occasionally utilize these techniques; however, I am not consistent in implementing these techniques. I may need additional support.
- **Proficient**
  - o I am very skilled in this area, and I utilize these techniques in the classroom with some positive outcomes with students.
- **Exemplary**
  - o I am an expert in this area, and I consistently utilize these techniques in the classroom with significant student results.

THE CIRCLE OF ACTION

Once you have rated your skills in a specific area, the next step is taking action to make improvements. In working with my clients over the years, I have witnessed great success through the use of the Circle of Action, shown below. This tool helps you implement change through the assessment of four areas:

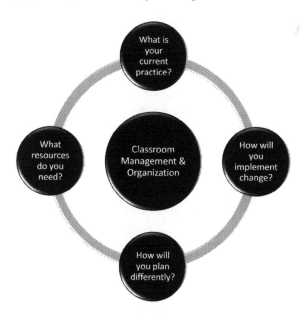

- **What Is Your Current Practice?**
  - o Here you will outline the current process or the outcome of an event. Write down what went (or is going) right and what went (or is going) wrong, as well as any other pertinent details.
- **How Will You Implement Change?**
  - o Here you will pinpoint the specific areas that need improvement, as well as the means through which you will bring about the change.
- **How Will You Plan Differently?**
  - o Once you have an outline of the changes you would like to make, the next step is to create a process to implement the changes. This could include research, timelines, milestones, and action steps.
- **What Resources Do You Need?**
  - o In order to enact these changes, determine if you will require additional training, materials, assistance from a colleague, or leadership intervention. By outlining your required resources, you can enact a plan to acquire them.

THE DESERT ISLAND

Before we delve into the main chapters, I would like to start with an exercise I conduct with my clients.

Imagine that a ship you are on is sinking. Fortunately, you can save yourself by swimming to a nearby desert island. The boat is sinking fast, and you only have time to grab one object before evacuating the boat.

Describe the object you would bring and why you would bring it.

Object: _____

Why I chose this object:

_____
_____
_____

This exercise resonates with educators because a classroom is a lot like a desert island. Once you're on the island, to survive, you have only the tools you brought with you.

As in this exercise, before you step onto your island, put some thought into the tools you'll take with you.

What do I mean by *tools*? Coming into each day with your lessons properly prepared. Making sure to have extra supplies on hand in case a student forgets something. Keeping an extension cord and device charger in your drawer in the event a student's tablet or laptop runs out of batteries. Putting contingencies in place if a lesson goes faster than planned and you wind up with extra time to fill.

Tools can also include the people you rely on. Especially in the early stages of our careers, we teachers tend to swim out to our islands alone without support or collaboration, when we really don't have to. There are many networks all around us we can take advantage of. Whether through our Instagram or Facebook friends or our team members at school, we can have more successful outcomes if we are not operating alone.

Ultimately, when assembling your desert island toolbox, make sure each tool is appropriate for the job and sharpened to a fine edge. The following chapters aim to help you in this task.

CHAPTER 1
ARE YOU SCURRYING TO THE FINISH?
Classroom Organization and Management

OVERVIEW

A classroom that runs like a perfectly oiled machine doesn't happen by accident. By the same token, teachers who instantly command the attention of their students are not magicians who simply have it all under control.

The truth is that effective classroom organization and management come down to learning the top research-based and field-tested strategies. Armed with these strategies, if you execute them properly, you can capture the interest of even the least-attentive scholars.

To that end, this chapter will fill your toolbox with things you need to manage diverse student learners in all learning environments.

CASE STUDY

I entered a middle school classroom to find a chaotic environment that seemed more like recess than instructional time. Students were physically sitting in clusters facing one another, and everyone was talking loudly. Needless to say, no one was paying attention to the frazzled-looking teacher standing in the front of the classroom.

Sitting in the back of the classroom, I shot a quick video of the moment and then observed the teacher's lesson until the class period was over.

During the changing of classes, I asked the teacher if we could quickly rearrange the desks in more traditional rows. As we did so, I described to the teacher a series of proven strategies to effectively steer students toward a mindset suited for learning. In other words, I outlined methods to capture their attention and keep it.

As the next class filed into the classroom for the new class period, I created a circle of respect and enthusiasm as students entered. I walked around the classroom smiling and repeating, "Welcome, students! Let's get ready for success!" I asked them all to have a seat and get ready for success. They all looked bewildered yet intrigued by this stranger standing in their classroom and telling them to get ready for success. Once all the students were seated and ready, I introduced myself and set the tone for class. I used many of the strategies I will share with you in this book, and I demonstrated some of these methods to the teacher before handing the reins back to her. I later resumed my seat in the back of the class to observe the next lesson. I took another video. This time, students were attentive and eager to learn. In fact, the difference between the two classes before and after intervention was so stark that frankly, the videos looked staged— almost too good to be true.

The good news is that these results are not too good to be true! When provided with the proper learning environment, students will instantly become more engaged. Best of all, it's not magic. This approach involves passion, science, and psychology that every teacher can harness.

CLASSROOM FLOW AND ARRANGEMENT

Let's begin by setting our intention before we continue with this chapter. What exactly are you looking to gain with regard to managing your classroom environment? Do you know what your needs might be? In the case study I just shared, the teacher had no intention because she had not analyzed the needs. In the process, we discovered that she needed to gain a sense of order and rapport with her students.

Consider for a moment a fast food restaurant. Imagine how long it would take to get your food if the kitchen was across the parking lot, the freezer was in the main building, and the cleaning supplies were kept behind the register. To make matters worse, imagine there was no specific employee assigned to fill soft drinks or cook food or a process in place for making a sandwich or operating the appliances.

This may seem like a silly analogy, but the point here is that to efficiently take your food order and turn it into a meal, the restaurant would need better flow and arrangement. It would need a kitchen located near the counter, ingredients stored within easy reach of the cooks, clearly defined roles among the staff, and processes that were faithfully executed until they became second nature to all involved (including the customers).

In a classroom, flow and arrangement pertain not to burgers and fries but to the flow of information and skills you intend to teach.

Flow

In the context of this book, *flow* means considering the activities at hand (lectures, group projects, individual projects, exams, and so on); optimizing your lesson plans to follow a logical sequence of events; making smooth transitions between activities; and establishing daily rituals and routines so the students always know what to expect. Whether you are teaching in a virtual environment, tutoring one on one, or conducting a traditional lesson, it is essential to create an effective flow for the class. It will help students understand their learning goals each day and give them order as they process new information.

Ultimately, you have to put rituals and routines in place to effectively create classroom flow. In other words, students will perform at their best and respect the process of learning when there is order and each day is organized.

Arrangement

Classroom arrangement goes hand in hand with classroom flow. Just like the fast food restaurant, to serve up some burgers (your lesson plan), you need:

- a clean and organized establishment,

- supplies that are fully stocked,
- ingredients within easy reach,
- a menu for the day, and
- a logical layout to efficiently and effectively deliver your product to your customers (the students).

In practice, this means putting a good deal of thought into making sure that you are not short on classroom essentials, such as laptops, iPads, Chromebooks, and class visuals, and that you don't need to fish around in a drawer for something if you run out. If you are using tablets or laptops, be certain to have a system in place to provide power to a student who forgot to charge his or her device overnight. Perhaps most importantly, the classroom needs to be arranged in a manner so that the instant a student sits down, he or she knows exactly what the activities will be for the day and understands precisely what he or she will be expected to do over the course of the lesson. We will go into specifics in the "Strategies for Success" section below.

Putting Flow and Arrangement into Practice

In the case study, the primary problems stemmed from a lack of classroom flow and arrangement. The arrangement was not optimal because students were sitting in clusters as the instructor was trying to teach a lesson at the front of the class. While clusters and pods are appropriate for some activities, they were challenging for that particular situation. The students were more interested in socializing with one another (naturally) and not positioned to receive information from the teacher. We addressed the need first by setting a tone for success and productivity and then by changing the seating arrangement to shift the focus of the students away from one another and toward the teacher.

Once this was accomplished, we took steps to create flow. Specifically, this meant addressing each student individually as he or she filed into the room, informing the students of what they needed to do when they got to their desks (e.g., open a book to a specific chapter), and asking each student to acknowledge if he or she was ready for success. This gave the students an opportunity to fully understand what was expected and encouraged a behavior of productivity.

With our world steadily evolving due to the COVID-19 pandemic as well as new technological advancements, we also must ask ourselves how this concept works in a virtual classroom setting.

When teaching and learning remotely, do you still need to be concerned with flow and arrangement? The answer is most definitely.

As you dive deeper into planning for instruction, you must also plan based on the learning environment. For example, if you find yourself teaching in a virtual setting, consider the ways you can arrange the flow to ensure effective instruction. Instead of standing and greeting students upon entering the physical classroom, you might be online, admitting students and greeting them as they enter the virtual classroom.

The challenges that manifest with virtual learning may at times be beyond your control, so be great at what you have control over. Ask yourself, *Is every student's computer working properly? Do I need to adjust for any students who are not able to participate virtually? Am I utilizing techniques to ensure all students are participating and maintaining attention on the lesson?* As you plan for success, always consider the variables and obstacles that may arise as a challenge, and use these strategies to create solutions.

MAXIMIZING STUDENT BEHAVIOR

In everyday classrooms, many teachers—whether they are veterans or novices—struggle with the ability to control student behavior. It is extremely important to develop, adopt, and implement routines; set clear expectations; and employ strategies that keep students engaged and on task.

STRATEGIES FOR SUCCESS (WHAT REALLY WORKS)

If you don't take anything else from this chapter, these are the things you should do to optimize student engagement and behavior.

Establish Routines and Rituals

As you begin to work in this space, it is important to define routines versus rituals. A routine is a procedure or process you implement regularly to establish order and consistency. A ritual is more ceremonial to help with social emotional well-being. Rituals have a more internal meaning, while routines have more of an external focus.

- **Explain and implement daily routines** until they become habits for you and your students. Examples include the following:
  o Before the students enter your classroom, post your daily agenda and targets on your smartboard as well as your online platform.
  o Put the class in the proper mindset by asking each student individually if he or she is ready for success and prepared to learn. This is powerful!
  o Clearly communicate targets and goals for the lesson before it begins.
- **Create rituals** to help students know what is expected of them. Examples can include the following:
  o "Lights off" means everyone is quiet.
  o Music or certain sounds (e.g., a bell) signal a transition from one activity to another.
  o Give virtual or real thumbs-ups.
- Define and **implement a set of classroom rules**.
- Make sure your students fully **understand your expectations for behavior**. What is acceptable in some classes may not be acceptable in others.
- Where appropriate, **empower your students to have input into the rules**. Help them learn to take ownership.

- **Use timers** to stay on schedule.
- **Be consistent** with your schedules, routines, and rituals.

Create Opportunity Instead of Punishment

- Ensure your students understand the consequences of inappropriate behavior.
- Provide ongoing opportunities to engage parents.
- Provide opportunities for students to learn from any inappropriate action.
- Offer parents the opportunity to help (for example, to volunteer).

Create a Culture and Climate of Success

People like to feel a sense of accomplishment and success. Each day, ensure that your students feel a sense of pride in themselves and in what they are learning. As you create these opportunities for success for your students, embrace success for yourself as well, and remember, falling is a part of success.

- Are you at 100 percent?

  This is the question we start with each day. Ask yourself, and then ask your students. Having 100 percent means engaging the entirety of a student's attention, understanding, cooperation, comprehension, and effort. In other words, both the teacher and the student are giving 100 percent effort to create, develop, and plan for success.

- Teach students how to collaborate.

  Human beings are created to coexist, work together, and depend on each other. We often miss the opportunity to help students grow because they have not learned how to collaborate with one another. Provide your scholars with a system for collaborating by giving them norms for collaborating, roles when working together, and outcomes for the collaboration.

- Collaborate with fellow teachers where appropriate.

Just as students are more successful and confident when working together, the same applies for teachers. There is much to gain by working with your colleagues, whether it's a new student teacher who is interning or a veteran teacher on staff. Learn the strengths and opportunities of your colleagues, and work together to plan lessons, interventions, social events, and more.

- Foster situations in which students are able to experience success each day.

Be intentional each day as to how each student will experience success. Create a success guide or journal each week for your students, and allow them to see and track their success. Allow students to have input in this intentional plan for success. Let them know that failure is not an option, and falling is not equivalent to failure. Give students the proper context to overcome an obstacle or challenge. This helps students become self-reliant as they build confidence in taking risks and learning from an error or challenge. Don't penalize students for an error; instead, offer them an opportunity to grow from it.

Build Self-Efficacy

As the old adage says, "You are what you eat." Therefore, we must recognize what we are "feeding" ourselves as well as our students. Creating an effective classroom begins with students who believe in themselves. As we learn to feed positive desires and minimize negative influences, we can help students build positive perceptions about their lives and learning.

- Teach your students to think about it.

Effective teaching goes far beyond memorization of facts. The ultimate goal is for your students to learn how to think, focus, solve problems, and use their collective intelligence to its fullest. What does this mean? Students often are not learning because they are not thinking. Therefore, strive to teach your students how to think about what they are learning. Teach them to focus (versus letting their minds wander). There is incredible power in focused thinking. Teach them that they have the power to control their thoughts and their focus. Similar to how meditation can help adults relieve stress and tackle big problems, students who focus their efforts on learning can accomplish more.

- Set a healthy expectation for challenges.

Let students know ahead of time that part of your master plan is to challenge them, but the challenges should engage them and create an opportunity to work together and grow together. Be sure to properly challenge students based on their individual readiness. Remember, the goal is to create moments of success with them.

- Show and model for students how to ask meaningful questions.

Often, norms are not created for students to ask questions. Create norms for students to feel comfortable asking questions of you and one another. If done properly from the start, this can be a huge opportunity for students to increase their critical-thinking abilities.

- Promote a healthy lifestyle.

There are many variables to consider when we consider confidence in ourselves. Research shows that people who exercise and eat well have more energy and better health. Helping students define themselves and believe in their abilities cannot be done without a focus on mental, emotional, and physical health. While you may not be a fitness trainer or social worker, you can create and promote wellness routines in your class that help students feel good about themselves.

Teach at a High Level

As we get to the heart of what really works, there is no substitute for high-level instruction. Students deserve to be taught well. They are our future, and it's in our best interest to teach them at high levels. In order to consistently provide high-level, engaging instruction, you need to implement the following strategies:

- Spend the appropriate time planning your lessons.
- Study your content. Be current in your research and practice.
- Make sure materials are ready before each class.
- Facilitate activities to ensure your students stay engaged.
- Establish and uphold daily benchmarks for learning.
- Continually assess yourself as a teacher, and seek ways to improve.

Remove Distractions

The task of removing distractions goes without saying, but it can often be complex and should be approached from a proactive standpoint as much as possible. Effective teachers and leaders plan for distractions and create solutions before the distractions manifest.

- Identify and eliminate classroom disruptions.
    - Separate students who are prone to talking to one another, or give them roles for class to keep them focused on learning tasks and leadership roles.
    - Remove any unnecessary items that may be distracting for students.
    - Set norms for devices, such as iPads, cell phones, smart watches, and tablets, so students clearly understand the expectations

for use in your class. Share this norm with parents to ensure everyone is clear and on the same page.

- Create a classroom culture that yields learning.
  - o Have you created an environment that's conducive to learning? Do students subconsciously see your classroom as a place to get things done or a place to talk to their friends? What kind of tone do you set when they enter your classroom?
- Strive to be a positive teacher each and every day.
  - o Again, feed yourself with inspiring information so you can transfer that to your students. They need it, and so do you!

When students miss the mark for behavioral expectations, how do you respond? What is your plan? As you continue to strengthen your classroom muscles, you will become more effective at managing classroom behavior.

Identify Causes for Misbehavior

- Are the students bored?
- Are the students hungry?
- Is a child hurt or sick?
- Is there a special need to consider?

Once you identify the underlying cause(s) for the undesirable behavior, address the situation in isolation, and engage the parents or guardians as soon as possible. Please note that this should not be the only time you engage with families. By the time engagement regarding misbehavior happens, you should have a well-established relationship. Your attempts with the student will prosper if you have developed a positive bridge between yourself and the family.

Understand Your Teaching Style

Knowing who you are in the classroom is essential to managing the overall process. Do you know your teaching style? Are you a delegator?

Authoritarian? Facilitator? What is your educational philosophy? What do you enjoy most about teaching?

Pause, think, and reflect: What is my teaching style? What do I enjoy most about teaching?

_____

_____

_____

_____

_____

_____

Now that you have considered your most effective self, here are a few strategies to better analyze yourself as a teacher.

- Record and watch a video of yourself teaching.
- Identify the teaching or management style that feels most natural to you.
    - o   Know its strengths and advantages.
    - o   Know its potential pitfalls and challenges.
- Routinely assess your behavior (self-reflect).
- When communicating with students, strive to always use proper grammar.
- Monitor your body language.
- Care about the quality of instruction you are giving.

Once you have taken the steps outlined above, develop your lesson (action) plan. Make sure the lesson plan:

- is student-centered,
- offers clear rules and expectations,
- has exciting incentives, and
- engages parents and guardians in a positive way.

EVALUATION AND SELF-REFLECTION

Developing	I am aware, but I really don't utilize these techniques like I should and I need additional support.
Competent	I am aware, and I occasionally utilize these techniques, however, I am not consistent with implementing these techniques. I may need additional support.
Proficient	I am very skilled in this area, and I utilize these techniques in the classroom with some positive outcomes with students.
Exemplary	I am an expert in this area, and I consistently utilize these techniques in the classroom with significant student results.

Notes:

_____

_____

_____

_____

_____

_____

_____

_____

_____

_____

_____

_____

_____

_____

_____

_____

_____

_____

_____

_____

_____

_____

Tova Davis, Ed.D.

The following are pertinent questions to ask yourself when evaluating your classroom management and organization. Please rate or evaluate yourself on the following.

Classroom Organization and Management

Classroom Flow	Classroom Organization	Student Behavior	Time on Task
Daily routines, rituals, movement	Classroom arrangement, Clean, Free of excess papers	PBIS? Proactive discipline plan, Consistent consequences	Total time teaching
Developing ☐	Developing ☐	Developing ☐	Developing ☐
Competent ☐	Competent ☐	Competent ☐	Competent ☐
Proficient ☐	Proficient ☐	Proficient ☐	Proficient ☐
Exemplary ☐	Exemplary ☐	Exemplary ☐	Exemplary ☐

Is my classroom clean, neat, and organized?			
Developing ☐	Competent ☐	Proficient ☐	Exemplary ☐

Do I efficiently transition my students from one task to the next?			
Developing ☐	Competent ☐	Proficient ☐	Exemplary ☐

Have I established classroom rituals and routines that are nonnegotiable? Are my students aware?			
Developing ☐	Competent ☐	Proficient ☐	Exemplary ☐

Do I change my classroom environment to creatively support the lesson?			
Developing ☐	Competent ☐	Proficient ☐	Exemplary ☐

Is my classroom a well-managed, safe environment that encourages respect, positivity, and growth for all learners?			
Developing ☐	Competent ☐	Proficient ☐	Exemplary ☐

Do I create a student-centered academic environment in which teaching and learning occur at high levels and students are self-directed learners?			
Developing ☐	Competent ☐	Proficient ☐	Exemplary ☐

Circle of Action: Classroom Management and Organization

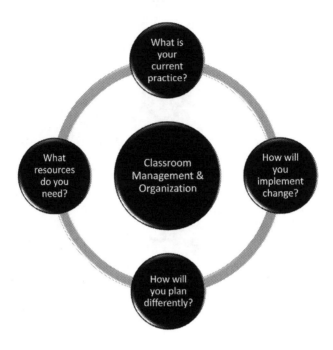

What is your current practice?

_____

_____

_____

How will you implement change?

_____

_____

_____

How will you plan differently?

_____

_____

_____

What resources do you need?

_____

_____

_____

ADDITIONAL RESOURCES

- Robert J. Marzano and Jana S. Marzano have outlined a series of tenets in their "The Key to Classroom Management." These stem from "research-based strategies combining appropriate levels of dominance and cooperation and an awareness of student needs." Using these tenets, "teachers can build positive classroom dynamics." You can find this resource by visiting http://www.ascd.org/publications/educational-leadership/sept03/vol61/num01/The-Key-to-Classroom-Management.aspx.
- If you would like to explore additional classroom management strategies, an excellent resource is "Best Practices in Classroom Management," written by Christopher Dunbar from the College of Education at Michigan State University. You can find it by visiting http://www.innovativeeducatorsforum.org/Best_practices/Best%20Practices%20in%20Class%20room.pdf.

CHAPTER 2
A MARATHON OR A SPRINT?
Instructional Planning and Delivery

OVERVIEW

Imagine you are watching a politician deliver an inspiring speech, a stand-up comedian roast a heckler in the back row, or your school's principal inspire the student body during a graduation. Regardless of the setting or context, it's hard not to marvel at the way an expert speaker can take command of a room, get his or her message clearly across, and make an impact.

The truth is, that ease you witnessed was actually the result of practice and preparation. Yet somehow, a large number of educators harbor the misconception that teachers can wing it and still deliver an effective lesson plan.

Instead, teachers who phone it in when it comes to lesson planning are met with disaster when they get in front of their students. Predictably, poor lesson plans result in substandard instruction. Lesser-known negative impacts of poor lesson planning include a lack of student engagement, behavioral issues, and learning loss.

Effects of Poor Lesson Planning

- Substandard instruction
- Lack of student engagement
- Potential for behavioral issues

The purpose of this chapter will be to walk you through the proven, time-tested best practices for successful instructional planning and delivery. Sure, following these processes will entail slightly more effort than winging it, but the end results will be a more engaged class and significantly improved delivery.

WHY INSTRUCTIONAL PLANNING AND DELIVERY ARE IMPORTANT

The concepts discussed in this chapter are similar to planning an event. You must begin with the end in mind. Think about the details that must be considered to plan a wedding or birthday party. The planner must consider the number of guests, location, catering, decor, music, budget, and so on to have a successful event. All of the small details must be worked out well before guests arrive.

The Classroom Is a Stage

Another way to think of instructional planning is from the viewpoint of an actor or actress, a rock star, or perhaps the conductor of a symphony. The performance actually started months before the performer hit the stage in terms of the time he or she spent planning and rehearsing. To the audience, the show may look improvised, but the performer knows that a great deal of thought and effort went into achieving a natural and pleasing rhythm to the performance.

The rhythm of the classroom is no different from that of a concert. You need to draw the audience in and then hold their attention through an engaging ebb and flow of energy. Using proper instructional planning techniques will help you find that rhythm to keep your class riveted throughout the course of your lesson.

Owning the Classroom

Whether or not the stage metaphors mentioned above resonate with you, we can all agree that an effective teacher needs to own the classroom.

Owning the classroom means being accountable for—among many other things—the content in the classroom. In order for you as a teacher to be effective in the classroom, you must understand the value of creating effective plans and delivering those plans with creativity and purpose. Take a genuine responsibility for the lives that sit before you. Take time to understand the value that you alone can add to your students' future. In taking ownership of our classrooms, we become intentional with our thoughts, plans, and actions daily. The passion that parallels with owning your classroom often renders intangible outcomes.

Components of Effective Planning and Delivery

Whether you are planning for a traditional lesson, virtual classroom, or new digital platform, effective planning and delivery can be achieved through focus in the following areas:

- content preparation,
- collaborative planning,
- differentiation, and
- effective (and appropriate) use of technology.

The following sections of this chapter will break down the specifics of each of these areas before discussing ways for you to incorporate them into your own lesson planning.

CONTENT PREPARATION (UNPACKING THE STANDARDS)

Practically everything an educator does is ultimately to uphold an educational standard. In the consistent framework or in the broadest sense, a standard is always created to prepare a student for the next level in his or her education. Simply put, it is a guide that measures students' achievements at intervals during their educational process.

The specifics of the standards will depend not only on the grade level but also on the subject, as well as the state in which the educational institution resides. As a teacher, you are well aware of the standards you must uphold in your state for your grade and subject(s).

For the sake of context, here is an example of a Georgia standard, which specifically pertains to high school English: "Cite strong and thorough textual evidence to support analysis of what the text says explicitly as well as inferences drawn from the text, including determining where the text leaves matters uncertain" (Georgia Department of Education).

Why am I quoting a random example of a standard in a subject you may or may not teach in a state you may or may not teach in? To illustrate how every lesson plan needs to start by unpacking the standards with which to meet the educational goals your class (and you) are expected to master.

In unpacking this standard, we know the following:

- The students are required to read a literary work.
- Through effective instruction, the teacher will help the students effectively understand
  - the overall plot,
  - explicit details,
  - inferences,
  - frame narratives,
  - structure and detail, and
  - citations and textual evidence when forming an argument.

Now, when the teacher creates this lesson plan, every aspect of the plan needs to work backward from the overarching goals outlined in this standard.

Some students in your class may be excellent and enthusiastic readers. Others might dislike reading. Some students may exhibit high levels of reading comprehension. Others might need thorough explanations of concepts or some fun exercises and engaging projects to help them understand the more complex details within the analysis. In other words, one size won't fit all, and the lesson plan should reflect the variety of learners and learning styles present in the classroom. So how do we accomplish that?

REVIEW YOUR DATA

It is important for a teacher to use data when building an effective lesson plan. Why? Let's say, for example, you teach a woodshop class but recently changed school districts. Your previous school district was located in a rural area where students typically picked up a basic working knowledge of woodworking tools and techniques from observing their parents fix things around the farm. In your new school district, which is located in a suburban area, the students are generally unfamiliar with the basics of woodworking. Would this change how you approach your lesson plan? Of course it would.

That's why the first step in any effective lesson plan should be collecting pertinent data about who your students are and what they need. How do you do that? Here are some examples of effective ways to collect data:

- interest surveys or interviews,
- prior test scores,
- evaluation of prior homework assignments, and
- one-on-one conversations with the students.

Once you have collected data, carefully analyze your various data sources, and then use your findings to tailor your lesson plans to the specific needs of your students.

Note that this isn't a one-and-done type of exercise. It's important to continuously collect data so you can fine-tune your lesson plans on a continuous basis. For example, if fifteen out of twenty students miss a specific question on a test or homework assignment, determine why. Assess what their needs are, and create a plan that addresses the problem and fills the learning gaps. Don't penalize the students. Make it a learning opportunity.

VALUE COLLABORATION

Suppose you have a seasoned colleague who has taught in your school district for upward of fifteen years. Since he first started, he has seen the school in which you teach triple in size. He's also worked under four different principals and three superintendents, each of whom possessed a different philosophy about education. You also have a colleague who is fresh out of school, and she's well versed in all the most up-to-date educational research and teaching techniques. Meanwhile, you have taught in four different school districts in three different states, ranging from urban to rural settings. Don't let that collective knowledge go to waste!

Collaborative planning is an evidence-based practice in which teachers can pool their expertise, leverage each other's unique experiences, and ultimately create an elaborate toolbox to deliver more effective instruction. Instead of operating in a silo, best practices require you to team up with your colleagues to work cooperatively on tasks and projects for maximum benefit to your students. Here are some examples of how to effectively collaborate.

- Share information with your teammates, including
  - lesson plans,
  - test scores,
  - resources,
  - past experiences, and
  - pertinent information about students.
- Utilize the process of collaborating to determine opinions and beliefs and explore attitudes and decision-making practices.
- Analyze achievements in the context of standards.
- Review and edit each other's lesson plans, and make suggestions for improvements.

In short, not following a collaborative planning process represents a significant missed opportunity to maximize the potential of your lessons.

DIFFERENTIATE

As we continue to engage in the blueprint for effective instructional planning and delivery, there is no way around the ability to meet students where they are. If we are really planning to have successful outcomes for students, the focus has to be on their specific needs. Using the data we have about our students, we must differentiate our instructional delivery. What is differentiated instruction? It is the ability to vary teaching strategies to meet the needs of all students through the content we teach, the process we use to deliver the content, and the outcome or product we strive to have. Differentiating involves understanding how students learn and, in turn, creating lessons that accommodate their intellectual abilities. Carol Tomlinson, differentiated-instruction expert and author, says that differentiation is:

- qualitative;
- rooted in assessment;
- a combination of multiple approaches to content, process, and product;
- student-centered;
- a blend of instruction to the whole class, smaller groups, and individuals; and
- organic.

So what does this mean in context? In other words, how would the parameters provided in the above list directly affect how you construct a lesson plan to meet the needs of your class? If your class is reading of *The Merchant of Venice*, here are some concrete examples.

- **Differentiating content**: Provide access to multiple versions of *The Merchant of Venice* to cater to your range of students and their capacities to learn. Since some students will have no trouble in comprehending the original version, while others may need a fair amount of translation and explanation, giving your students the text in varying forms will better enable students of different abilities to meet the corresponding standard.

- **Differentiating process**: Alter the activity to better enable students to learn. For example, devise a game that helps with comprehension of the language, have students perform a scene from the play, assign students to write a poem about the play, create work stations and have students rotate through each station, and perform tasks designed to assist with comprehension.

- **Differentiating product**: This pertains to the various ways in which a student can demonstrate mastery of a standard. Examples can include a written exam, presentation, journal, portfolio, and more.

- **Learning environment**: Reconfigure the physical environment based on the project and what may best enhance learning. Examples can include arranging the classroom as a theater so students can act out scenes from *The Merchant of Venice*, turning the lights down and playing jazz music for poetry readings, or using movable wall panels to create quiet spaces to work on group projects. The goal is to find creative ways to set up the classroom environment to complement the activity and optimize learning.

It's important to remember that when exploring differentiation, the goal is always to meet the learners' needs.

EFFECTIVE (AND APPROPRIATE) USE OF TECHNOLOGY

Now, as we work to meet students' needs and be intentional about our outcomes, think about the last time you went on a hike, bike ride, or adventure of some sort with your friends. Did you notice that one friend had *all* the gear—a hydration pack, a GPS, a first-aid kit, trekking poles, $350 boots, and pretty much everything needed for exploration in the mountains—even though you were only walking two miles on a nature path behind your school?

While there is a place and time for those tools and gadgets, in some instances, unnecessary gear just weighs you down, adds complexity, and detracts from the simple pleasure of walking among nature.

The same holds true with regard to technology in the classroom. Don't gear up for an arctic expedition (figuratively speaking) when a water bottle, some sunscreen, and a comfy pair of shoes are all you need. In a nutshell, do the following:

- Use only the appropriate technology needed to support the lesson.
- Make sure the technology attached to the lesson is enhancing the student experience and represents effective use.
  - o Reading *The Merchant of Venice* on a tablet is an effective use.
  - o Having students in your literature class program Ozobots to act out a scene from *The Merchant of Venice* is awesome, but make sure the activity lends itself to meeting the standards.
- Don't perpetuate the screenager phenomenon. Make sure lessons that utilize technology are also designed for interaction, both between you and the students and, where appropriate, among the students.
- Explore new digital lesson-planning tools. There are many ways to virtually build, learn, and collaborate with your team using electronic platforms.
- As with other components of your lesson plan, the goal is always to hit the learning target and meet the standard.

STRATEGIES FOR SUCCESS (WHAT REALLY WORKS)

If you don't take anything else from this chapter, these are the things that will optimize instructional planning and delivery.

Build Self-Efficacy

- Every student is smart in his or her own way. It's your job to show them all how smart they are.
- Compose your lesson plans in ways to leverage students' strengths and improve upon areas of weakness.
  - o Unravel the mystery of how your students like to learn, and adapt your activities accordingly.
  - o Find creative ways to help students work past mental roadblocks (for example, by using music to help them with language comprehension).
- Strive to foster a feeling of accomplishment every day that will build your students' confidence and make them excited to learn.

Teach at a High Level

- Spend the appropriate time planning your lessons.
- Rehearse your lesson.
- Visualize your success.
- Continually refer back to the standards to ensure your lesson plan will meet your educational goals.
- Leverage the expertise of your colleagues to ensure the best possible lesson plans.
- Continually assess your lesson plans, and seek ways to improve.

EVALUATION AND SELF-REFLECTION

Developing	I am aware, but I really don't utilize these techniques like I should and I need additional support.
Competent	I am aware, and I occasionally utilize these techniques, however, I am not consistent with implementing these techniques. I may need additional support.
Proficient	I am very skilled in this area, and I utilize these techniques in the classroom with some positive outcomes with students.
Exemplary	I am an expert in this area, and I consistently utilize these techniques in the classroom with significant student results.

Notes:

The following are pertinent questions to ask yourself when evaluating your instructional planning and delivery. Please rate or evaluate yourself on the following.

Do you spend time deconstructing or unpacking the standard(s) being taught?			
Developing ☐	Competent ☐	Proficient ☐	Exemplary ☐
Do you spend ample time researching and planning your lessons and activities?			
Developing ☐	Competent ☐	Proficient ☐	Exemplary ☐
Do you plan with colleagues?			
Yes ☐		No ☐	
Do you plan for differentiation by developing various levels of delivery?			
Developing ☐	Competent ☐	Proficient ☐	Exemplary ☐
Are your lessons and activities engaging, student-centered, and creative?			
Yes ☐		No ☐	
Do your lessons stretch the imagination of students or simply cover material?			
Developing ☐	Competent ☐	Proficient ☐	Exemplary ☐
Are you considering all forms of intelligence, strengths, and weaknesses?			
Yes ☐		No ☐	
Do you provide time for reteaching and enrichment?			
Yes ☐		No ☐	
Do you plan with rigor in mind?			
Yes ☐		No ☐	
What data do you use when developing each lesson plan?			
Do you appropriately plan and utilize technology?			
Yes ☐		No ☐	

Instructional Planning & Delivery

Content Preparation	Collaborative Planning	Differentiation	Appropriate Use of Technology
Use of essential questions, unpacking standards	Working with other teachers and school leaders	Planning various activities for understanding in content process, and product	Appropriate apps, games, devices. Trained in usage of instructional technology to improve classroom instruction
Developing ☐	Developing ☐	Developing ☐	Developing ☐
Competent ☐	Competent ☐	Competent ☐	Competent ☐
Proficient ☐	Proficient ☐	Proficient ☐	Proficient ☐
Exemplary ☐	Exemplary ☐	Exemplary ☐	Exemplary ☐

Circle of Action: Instructional Planning and Delivery

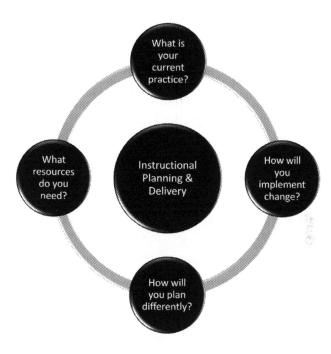

What is your current practice?

_____

_____

_____

How will you implement change?

_____

_____

_____

How will you plan differently?

_____

_____

_____

What resources do you need?

_____

_____

_____

ADDITIONAL RESOURCES

Content Preparation and Unpacking the Standards

- Former K–12 teacher and administrator Maria Nelson wrote about how unpacking standards fosters confidence in students. Learn more by visiting http://allthingsassessment.info/2016/07/19/unpacking-standards-leads-to-confidence-not-chaos-for-teachers-and-students/.
- A detailed overview of unpacking standards can be found by visiting https://pdo.ascd.org/lmscourses/PD12OC002/media/CCSS_UBD_M2_Reading_Unpacking_Standards.pdf.
- A helpful guide to breaking down standards into components can be found by visiting http://www.sau17.org/userfiles/-4/my%20files/deconstructingstandardssteps.pdf?id=63.

Collaborative Planning

- You can find the Georgia Department of Education's guidelines and expectations for collaborative planning at http://www.gadoe.org/School-Improvement/School-Improvement-Services/Documents/System%20for%20Effective%20School%20Instruction/GaDOE%20Collaborative%20Planning%20Expectations.pdf.

Differentiation

- https://journals.sagepub.com/doi/pdf/10.3102/0091732X188 21130.
- https://www.researchgate.net/publication/271406819_ Differentiated_Instruction_Making_Informed_Teacher_Decisions.

Technology

- An additional helpful guide to classroom technologies that increase learning can be found at https://www.highspeedinternet. com/resources/a-guide-to-classroom-technologies-that-increase-learning-an-educators-resource/.

CHAPTER 3
HOW DO YOU RELAY?
Effective Communication and Positive Relationships

OVERVIEW

When someone asks you for directions, what kind of directions do you give?

- Turn-by-turn directions using street names?
- A list of landmarks to look out for?
- Instructions to head in a certain direction for a specific number of miles before veering off in another direction?
- GPS coordinates?
- An address one can enter into a smartphone or navigation app?

As disparate as they are, all of these methods will likely get someone where he or she needs to go. However, there are two points to consider here:

1. You possess the ability to communicate the same information in a vast number of ways.
2. You may need to adapt the ways in which you communicate information to others to best suit their specific needs.

What do I mean? For example, an address to enter into a phone will be ideal for most people in most places but useless to someone on a country road out of cell phone range. Therefore, to best help that person, you would need to adapt your method of communication to make it as useful as possible for the situation.

Using this analogy, what type of directions do you provide when you communicate with people you encounter during a typical school day? Are you providing the necessary details? Are you taking into account the recipient's abilities and preferences? Does the message you're sending fit situational limitations that may be present?

The purpose of this chapter will be to discuss the significance of effective communication and the fostering of positive relationships and provide some suggestions on how to develop more effective communication. This chapter closes with some exercises to help you test your communication skills.

WHY EFFECTIVE COMMUNICATION IS IMPORTANT

For fun, imagine you are a visitor from another planet. Due to your superior intelligence, not to mention experience and knowledge gleaned from eons of traveling the galaxy, you know the secret to human happiness.

You can't wait to tell everyone, but you run into a problem when you discover, predictably, no one can understand your language, facial expressions, or hand gestures. Sadly, your secret remains a secret.

Sure, this is a silly example, but the point is that even the most important information is useless if there is no way to effectively communicate it.

The same holds true in your terrestrial classroom. Poor communication will render even the best lesson plans ineffective. Therefore, your ability to communicate is crucial to your ability to educate.

Now that we have established the importance of effective communication, let's define what it is and how to use it to your advantage.

What Are the Forms of Communication?

Communication can be broken down into two primary forms: verbal and nonverbal.

- **Verbal communication** is generally considered to encompass speaking and writing.
- **Nonverbal communication** encompasses tone and pitch of the voice, facial expressions, body language, gestures, and other cues.

Needless to say, clear verbal communication is crucial, but the nonverbal elements have to be in place, or else your message can be misinterpreted. Consider these two examples:

- Imagine someone says, "I really like you" and accompanies the statement with a warm smile and a hug.
- Now imagine someone says, "I really like you," and accompanies the statement with an eye roll and an exasperated tone of voice.

In this example, the words are identical, but the meanings are completely different. This illustrates the vital role nonverbal communication plays and why it's so important that we are aware of not only the words we speak but also our tone of voice, facial expressions, and body language.

What Is Your Communication Style (and Why Does This Matter)?

In addition to maintaining an acute awareness of every facial expression and gesture you make, it is important to understand the roles that communication styles play in the effectiveness of our communication.

There are four primary communication styles that surfaced in the midst of my research on effective communication. These definitions taken directly from a presentation I viewed, explicitly define the four styles.

- **Expressive**
  - o "Expressives tend to be high energy, speak quickly, and focus on the big picture. They generally find conflict or differences

in opinion invigorating. People often perceive Expressives to seem overly cheerful, vain, or unpredictable."

- **Systematic**
  - o "Systematics focus on the facts and details and not on the big picture. They're generally not comfortable with conflict. People often perceive Systematics to seem unemotional or nonchalant."
- **Sympathetic**
  - o "Sympathetics like to focus on people and relationships, are good listeners and generally concerned with everyone's needs. They typically don't like conflict. People often perceive Sympathetics to seem soft-hearted or overly helpful. They also can be perceived as procrastinators when distracted."
- **Direct**
  - o "Directs are generally brief in conversation and often involved in many things at once. They tend to see the big picture and are more focused on the outcome than on the smaller tasks. People often perceive Directs to seem self-confident, intimidating, and opinionated."

These distinctions in style are important because they can create unintended conflict if we lack understanding of them. Consider the following examples.

Imagine a big-picture-driven direct person discussing a project with a detail-oriented systematic person. One is likely to get frustrated with the other for not focusing on what he or she deems the most important aspects of the project.

Now imagine an expressive person (who is high energy and thrives on conflict) discussing a project with a sympathetic (who is tenderhearted and avoids conflict).

Fortunately, as an education professional, you can proactively take steps to avoid conflicts in communication styles by doing the following:

1. Identify your personal communication style, and become aware of it.

2. Identify the communication styles of colleagues, students, parents, and others you interact with.

3. Strive to modify your communication as needed to better reach your audience. For example:

   - When speaking to a direct, focus on the outcome, not the minutiae.
   - When speaking to a systematic, dive into the details he or she sees as important.
   - When speaking to an expressive, try to increase your energy level, and don't be afraid to challenge him or her in a professional and courteous manner.
   - When speaking to a sympathetic, focus on his or her needs as well as building a relationship.

In summary, if you can master your words, tone, and body language as well as the nuances of the different communication styles, you can teach more effectively as well as work more effectively with your colleagues and supervisors.

WHY POSITIVE RELATIONSHIPS ARE IMPORTANT

Once you have improved your communication skills, the next step is to use your newfound abilities to build positive relationships.

Whether you're tasked with helping a student struggling with a difficult subject or convincing a parent to help ensure a student's homework gets done, your task is much easier when mutual trust and respect are present. In other words, if a student doesn't respect you, he or she will be less likely to do what you ask. If a parent doesn't trust in your knowledge and abilities, he or she will be less likely to take your assessments of and recommendations for his or her child seriously.

As such, building positive relationships represents a crucial step towards your success. Here's how to do it.

Identify Your Stakeholders

When you hear the word *stakeholder*, what do you think of? A stakeholder is anyone who is involved in or affected by a person's or an organization's actions. As such, we have stakeholders in all aspects of our lives. For example, our children are affected by our ability to provide food and shelter. Our spouses and significant others are involved in our happiness. For that matter, our summer-league softball team has a vested interest in our showing up on time each Thursday to play shortstop.

It's no different at your school. Many people are involved in or affected by what you do. These people include:

- students,
- parents,
- coworkers,
- school leaders, and
- community members.

Once you have identified your stakeholders, focus on the following to best build positive relationships.

Collaborate with Colleagues and Administration

Take time to create opportunities to work with your leaders and colleagues. Collaboration helps make everyone more effective through the sharing of skills, experiences, and knowledge. A welcome side effect is that collaboration also fosters strong relationships, much more so than operating in a silo.

Build Strong Teams

A great way to inspire collaboration is to build teams. For example, are you looking to improve the math curriculum among yourself and your fellow fourth-grade teachers? Create a team that includes your fellow teachers as well as, for example, a high school math teacher in your district, a local college professor, a member of the PTA who has an advanced degree in mathematics, perhaps a former student who went on to major in math in college, or anyone else in your sphere who would benefit the group. This will not only catalyze new ideas but also create a bond between team members that can be beneficial in other areas of your work.

Send Out Weekly Communications

Thanks to modern technology, parents and students can monitor scholastic performance in real time. Take advantage of this through frequent (and useful) communication. Whether through emails, newsletters, text alerts, or automated call systems, such as those offered by Google, not to mention more traditional methods, such as phone calls and written notes sent home with students, you have a great opportunity to build relationships with parents by keeping them informed.

A recommended approach would be to use a variety of communication methods and change up the days and times when the communications are sent. Doing so will better meet the needs of a varying audience who may have different schedules and preferences on how they want to receive information.

Also, avoid sending communications just to send communications. Always strive to include meaningful information as well as actionable items that provide students and parents the opportunity to ensure scholastic success.

Foster Parental Engagement and Involvement

Whether you teach first grade or tenth grade, it is essential for a parent to be not just engaged but also involved. What is the difference between engagement and involvement?

Engagement implies an emotional connection and a vested interest in the performance of a student, which you certainly want from a parent. Involvement implies something more proactive—in other words, not just caring about good grades but also working with the teacher to create an educational experience. In this way, having a parent in your corner can be a secret weapon to help a student perform at his or her best. Therefore, building strong relationships with students' parents is worthy of your efforts toward becoming a more effective educator.

Take a moment to reflect. How have you involved and engaged parents?

_____

_____

_____

_____

_____

STRATEGIES FOR SUCCESS (WHAT REALLY WORKS)

Here are some takeaways to optimize your communication style and relationship-building skills.

Foster an Environment for Effective Communication

- Create a community by building a culture in your school wherein effective communication is the norm and you are the example.
- Offer opportunities for students and parents to speak and voice their needs, thoughts, and feelings.
- Become the teacher leader who sets the tone for effective communication.
- Open up effective lines of communication with your stakeholders.
- Build positive relationships with your stakeholders to get everyone not only engaged but also involved.

Teach at a High Level

- Strive to always provide explicit information, which includes all the necessary details.

- Strive to communicate clearly and in ways that will prevent misinterpretation and confusion.
- Be mindful of how the information you provide is being received, and adjust your communication accordingly if needed.

INTERACTIVE EXERCISES

Exercise 1: Providing Directions

The way we communicate is essential to our success. Whether we are in the classroom or on the playground, the manner in which we communicate with our colleagues, supervisors, parents, and students determines how desirable our outcomes will be and if our goals will be reached. It's no different from being in a relationship with a spouse or significant other. No one can read our minds, so we have to be crystal clear when we provide guidance and instructions.

In this exercise, pretend someone asked you for directions to a grocery store or restaurant in your community. How specific would you be? What information about the person would you gather before providing an answer? Try it. Write it down.

_____

_____

_____

_____

_____

Did you list the name of the establishment you recommended? Did you list it first or last? Did you provide street names or just instruct the person to, for example, turn left and then turn right? Or did you simply provide an address and assume the person had a device to use GPS?

The takeaway of this exercise is that when we are communicating with students, parents, and stakeholders, we have to be deliberate in our communication; otherwise, people get lost. We have to consider our choice of words, our tone, and our nonverbal communication as well as the message. We also need to obtain information (data) sometimes before we can give our best response.

Exercise 2: Team Building

Are you the teacher leader or just a person who sits and waits for directives? Be honest!

Part 1: In this first part of this exercise, describe yourself as a team player. What have you done to contribute to the good of your team? What kinds of team-building efforts have you made lately?

_____

_____

_____

_____

_____

Part 2: If you are like most educators today, there is simply no time to do everything on your own. As with effective communication, creating an effective team is crucial to a successful classroom environment.

In the second part of this exercise, outline some ways to better foster teamwork between you and your colleagues.

_____

_____

_____

_____

_____

Exercise 3: Communication with Parents

Are you a teacher who leverages parents to help your students succeed, or are you simply keeping them informed on grades and a general idea of scholastic performance?

Part 1: In the first part of this exercise, assess your level of communication with parents. How often do you speak with students' parents? How often do you facilitate student conferences? Are you arming parents with the information they need to help ensure the success of their children?

_____

_____

_____

_____

_____

Part 2: There are many ways you can easily connect with parents on a weekly basis. Of course, these include the old-fashioned phone call and parent conference, but thanks to technology, there are many additional avenues at our disposal. These include emails, newsletters, text alerts, social media sites, and more.

In the second part of this exercise, outline some ways to better foster effective communication between yourself and the parents of your students.

_____

_____

_____

_____

_____

Exercise 4: Parental Engagement and Involvement

Once you have opened up lines of effective communication between yourself and your students' parents, you can create opportunities for parents to get engaged and involved on every level.

In this exercise, outline some steps you can proactively take to enhance engagement and foster involvement. Be intentional.

_____

_____

_____

_____

_____

Exercise 5: Collaboration with Colleagues and Administration

Remember the island in chapter 1? Don't allow your classroom to become an island!

In this exercise, reflect upon some ways to create opportunities to connect with your coworkers. Think in terms of helping to understand the process you all are going through together and how to leverage the wide range of skills and experiences each of you possesses.

_____

_____

_____

_____

_____

EVALUATION AND SELF-REFLECTION

Developing	I am aware, but I really don't utilize these techniques like I should and I need additional support.
Competent	I am aware, and I occasionally utilize these techniques, however, I am not consistent with implementing these techniques. I may need additional support.
Proficient	I am very skilled in this area, and I utilize these techniques in the classroom with some positive outcomes with students.
Exemplary	I am an expert in this area, and I consistently utilize these techniques in the classroom with significant student results.

Notes:

_____

_____

_____

_____

_____

_____

_____

_____

_____

_____

_____

_____

_____

_____

_____

_____

_____

_____

_____

_____

_____

_____

_____

_____

The following are pertinent questions to ask yourself when evaluating your effective communication and positive relationships. Please rate or evaluate yourself on the following.

Do you communicate rules and expectations to students and parents in a timely manner?			
Developing ☐	Competent ☐	Proficient ☐	Exemplary ☐

Do you send home weekly communications?			
Developing ☐	Competent ☐	Proficient ☐	Exemplary ☐

Do you communicate in all media to parents (e.g., email, text, hard copy, and automated call systems); in all languages spoken by the parents; and at various times?			
Developing ☐	Competent ☐	Proficient ☐	Exemplary ☐

Do you make yourself available to meet with parents?	
Yes ☐	No ☐

Do you work collaboratively with your colleagues and the administration?			
Developing ☐	Competent ☐	Proficient ☐	Exemplary ☐

Have you defined your communication style and your teaching style?	
Yes ☐	No ☐

Do you execute an effective incentive plan in class for students and parents?			
Developing ☐	Competent ☐	Proficient ☐	Exemplary ☐

Do you use encouraging verbal language and body language?	
Yes ☐	No ☐

Effective Communication & Positive Relationships

Team Building	Weekly Communication	Parental Engagement & Involvement	Collaboration w/ Colleagues & Administration
Activities for students and parents to build classroom community	Weekly progress reports, emails, texts, newsletters	Volunteering, assisting in class/ school events, inviting for visits, lunch	Collaborative planning, receptive to constructive feedbacks
Developing ☐	Developing ☐	Developing ☐	Developing ☐
Competent ☐	Competent ☐	Competent ☐	Competent ☐
Proficient ☐	Proficient ☐	Proficient ☐	Proficient ☐
Exemplary ☐	Exemplary ☐	Exemplary ☐	Exemplary ☐

**Circle of Action: Effective Communication and
Positive Relationships**

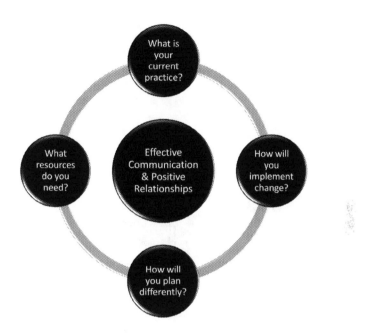

What is your current practice?

_____

_____

_____

How will you implement change?

_____

_____

_____

How will you plan differently?

_____

_____

_____

What resources do you need?

_____

_____

_____

ADDITIONAL RESOURCES

Parent Involvement and Engagement

- The Southwest Educational Developmental Laboratory published an extensive document entitled *A New Wave of Evidence: The Impact of School, Family, and Community Connections on Student Achievement*. Learn more by visiting http://www.sedl.org/connections/resources/evidence.pdf.

CHAPTER 4
WHO'S TRACKING?
Evaluating and Monitoring Student Learning

OVERVIEW

Thus far, we have discussed an array of effective, evidence-based methods to improve the quality of your instruction and, in turn, enhance the scholastic achievement of your students. Naturally, the first step in augmenting your effectiveness as an educator is to implement these meaningful improvements.

To recap, we have covered professional growth in the areas of:

- classroom organization and management,
- instructional planning and delivery, and
- effective communication and positive relationships.

If you have successfully made improvements in these areas, congratulations!

I, personally, am proud of your commitment to becoming a better teacher. In addition, I feel confident that the parents, your peers, and your school administrators appreciate your dedication. Most importantly, I am certain your students will benefit greatly from the improved instruction you provide, not only today but also in their future educational endeavors.

Considering the work you have accomplished, now probably seems like a good time to take a bit of a breather and enjoy your success, right? Not so fast! Making improvements is only half the battle. To fully realize your potential for success, there is another equally important element in your continual development as an instructor.

Specifically, now is the time to evaluate and monitor your progress and students' learning.

WHY EVALUATING AND MONITORING STUDENT LEARNING ARE IMPORTANT

When your doctor schedules a follow-up visit, it's not because he or she misses you; it's because your doctor is looking to see if your treatment is working.

If you report that you are feeling better, fantastic! Your doctor will likely conclude that he or she prescribed the correct medicine and gave the right advice. You will leave the office with a refill on your prescription and a directive to keep doing what you are doing with regard to rest, fluids, food, physical therapy, and so on.

If, however, you report that you are feeling the same or even worse, that means it's time for your doctor to do some additional fact-finding, reconsider his or her diagnosis, and likely explore some different treatment options.

As this chapter will illustrate, students also require follow-up visits from their teachers to ensure they are learning the concepts and ultimately meeting or exceeding the standards. As such, if you don't evaluate your progress and the progress of your students in a regular, systematic, and timely manner, you have no way to verify the effectiveness of your instruction and make necessary adjustments to optimize their potential.

With that in mind, the purpose of this chapter is to:

- discuss the use of data and its importance to effective instruction,
- outline the three traditional methods to collect data, and
- offer insights on how to use the data you collect to your advantage.

USE OF DATA

As you prepare to evaluate and monitor your students, it is essential to use multiple data sources. Simply put, data is any piece of factual information, such as a measurement or a statistic, you can leverage for the purpose of calculation, reasoning, or discussion.

What type of information do you typically gather, and how often?

_____

_____

Data can help you make informed decisions, plan more effectively, and much more. If your response to the above question was minimal, place a bookmark here to come back and respond again after you have finished the book.

Why is this an important discussion point? Each and every school day, whether you realize it or not, data (useful, valuable, actionable information) is presenting itself to you.

Here are some examples of actionable data that may have recently manifested within your classroom:

1. You noticed a student has been demonstrating uncharacteristically poor behavior.
2. You made a mental note of a group of normally attentive kids who suddenly have trouble concentrating.
3. You observed that the class seems more engaged when desks are arranged in a certain way.
4. You recognized an upward trend in test scores since you started sending more frequent communications to parents.

In truth, there probably isn't a minute that goes by when you are not presented with some piece of useful data. The question is, what are you doing with the data you are collecting?

To put it bluntly, if you are subconsciously or intentionally gathering all this information but aren't using it to your advantage, at best, you are teaching at a subpar level. At worst, you could be setting your students up for failure.

Let's revisit the examples above and hypothesize about potential courses of action.

1. **Student demonstrating poor behavior:** After some fact-finding, you determine the student who is exhibiting undesirable behavior is experiencing a personal problem that is affecting his or her scholastic performance.
   o As a course of action, you refer the student to the school's counselor for help.
2. **Students having trouble concentrating:** You learn that the group of normally attentive scholars have had a disagreement and have not worked together to resolve the issue.
   o As a course of action, you meet with them privately to help mediate and resolve their differences.
3. **Student engagement and seating arrangements:** After a little more experimentation, you determine conclusive correlations between seating arrangements and student engagement.
   o As a course of action, you apply the seating arrangements most conducive to student engagement for the remainder of the school year.
4. **Parent communication and test scores:** After some detailed analysis, you confirm the optimum times and methods for sending communications to parents.
   o As a course of action, you commit to sending out emails to parents on a specific day of every week, taking care to include clear instructions that can help their children succeed on upcoming tests and other projects.

Data can be your strongest ally in terms of guiding you on how to teach and reach your students and families. If you continue to chase your data and maintain a positive attitude about the data you're collecting and the actions you take as a result, you will see positive results.

ASSESSMENT TYPES

While a great deal of information can be gathered simply through observation, effective evaluation and monitoring require the adoption of proven best practices for gathering data. Following are three primary methods of data gathering in education:

1. **Diagnostic assessments**
2. **Formative assessments**
   - o Benchmark assessments (a subcategory of formative assessments)
3. **Summative assessments**

Diagnostic Assessments

- **What**: A diagnostic assessment determines what the learner already knows.
- **When**: The appropriate time to conduct a diagnostic assessment is before you start a new unit or introduce a new concept. Think of it as a pretest.
- **Why**: A diagnostic assessment empowers you to optimize the lesson based on the students' current level of knowledge and understanding.

Let's say you are teaching a course on the process of writing.

Before you begin the first lesson, if you ask your students what they already know about the basic steps of the process, their answers will guide how you approach the curriculum.

For example, if the students can easily recite the steps and demonstrate a clear understanding of each step, you can move forward with teaching some of the more advanced concepts. If not, you need to revisit the basic steps before moving forward.

Based on this example, the importance of the diagnostic assessment should be clear. Properly done, the assessment can

- prevent you from teaching advanced concepts to students who possess little chance of understanding the lesson or
- prevent you from boring your class with information they already know.

In other words, an effective diagnostic assessment empowers you to perfectly tailor the instruction to their current level of knowledge.

Diagnostic assessments can be conducted in a variety of manners. Here are some examples:

- observations
- surveys
- poignant questions
- one-on-one interviews with students
- portfolios (students put together creative portfolios regarding the concept, which could include pictures, short essays, maps, and more)
- quizzes

It's not vital which method you use to conduct a diagnostic assessment. There are multitudes of effective ways to informally assess aptitude and knowledge, and a method doesn't always have to use paper and pencil. The important thing is getting the students to express their level of understanding of a topic so you can configure your lessons accordingly.

Formative Assessments

- **What**: A formative assessment monitors student learning and progress.
- **When**: The appropriate time to conduct a formative assessment is during a lesson, unit, or chapter.
- **Why**: A formative assessment empowers you to make effective midlesson or midunit adjustments based on the students' demonstrated level of knowledge and understanding.

A formative assessment informs you, the teacher, where the students are right now in terms of knowledge, comprehension, and progress. It becomes an indicator that tells you how the work can be improved.

Following are some important attributes of formative assessments:

- They are ongoing. A formative assessment is always appropriate when a pulse check would be useful to gauge learning.
- Formative assessments provide an opportunity to reteach a topic if necessary.
- It's important that feedback to the students is a component of formative assessments, so students also have the opportunity to make adjustments if necessary and receive encouragement that they are successfully acquiring the targeted skills and information.
- Formative assessments should feel informal and nonthreatening to the students.

As with diagnostic assessments, there are many methods for gathering data. Here are some examples using a hypothetical process-of-writing lesson:

- Early in the lesson or unit, the students are asked to write down the five steps of the process from memory. The results will inform the teacher which students know the five steps (who is learning the basics of the process) and which students don't (who requires additional instruction or a different approach to the instruction before more advanced concepts can be introduced).
- Toward the latter part of the lesson, you could assign an activity in which the students apply the five steps to write a short essay or narrative. This will demonstrate if the students grasp the more advanced concepts (and are prepared to move forward) or if some of the concepts need to be revisited.

Using a variety of assessment methods provides huge amounts of actionable data that can inform the teacher on how best to proceed with a unit.

In fact, teachers who practice with formative assessments consistently have higher-performing students because these assessments give the teachers an opportunity to make adjustments to strategies and increase learning opportunities for students.

According to research cited by the National Council of Teachers of Mathematics, "Formative assessment produces greater increases in student achievement and is cheaper than other efforts to boost achievement, including reducing class sizes and increasing teachers' content knowledge."

Before we move on to the subcategory of formative assessments (benchmark assessments), here are some final thoughts on formative assessments as a whole:

- It's important to reiterate that students don't need to feel the pressure of an assessment. The goal is learning. It's not an "I got you; you didn't know it" opportunity. Don't penalize the students. The message should be "I've got your back, and I'm going to help you learn."
- In the context of a formative assessment, students should have a WOW (work on the work) moment.
- Formative assessments provide WOW opportunities for parents as well.
- Formative assessments are at their most effective when the teacher is giving constant, constructive, and descriptive feedback. In other words, the teacher is clearly communicating what students are doing well and what needs work, so they can improve.

Benchmark Assessments

One type of formative assessment that is common in the classroom is called a benchmark assessment. Also known as benchmark testing, it's an assessment type that gives the teacher more specific, quantifiable information on where the students are in terms of comprehension. It shows the mark, and there's typically a grade attached. A quiz represents a common type of benchmark assessment.

The important takeaway here, however, is that benchmark assessments focus on what the student is supposed to be learning and supposed to know by this time in the unit.

As you are well aware, there are an array of standards to be met. There are school-wide benchmarks, district-wide benchmarks, and state-wide standards, not to mention national standards.

Benchmark assessments offer you, the teacher, the opportunity to gauge your class's progress in relation to the standards you are responsible to uphold. Crucially, it gives you, the teacher, the opportunity to go back and reteach and avoid the risk of students falling behind.

Summative Assessments

- **What**: A summative assessment is used to assess student learning and progress after a unit has been completed.
- **When**: The appropriate time to conduct a summative assessment is at the end of the unit or semester.
- **Why**: A summative assessment empowers you to make adjustments to the curriculum so the curriculum is more effective the next time you teach a unit.

Summative assessments are given at the end of a quarter, semester, or school year. As noted above, their primary purpose is to assess the information the students should have learned throughout the course of a unit.

Examples of summative assessments include:

- final exams,
- final portfolios,
- essays, and
- reports.

Summative assessments will almost always be attached to a conclusive value, grade, or score that will indicate the level at which students absorbed the curriculum.

RETEACHING AND ENRICHMENT

Assessments are not always used for remediation. They should also be a source of information to create opportunities for students to grow. A key to effective teaching is the ability to recognize which students require reteaching and which could benefit from enrichment. Let's discuss what each is and how to implement these in your classroom.

Reteaching

As the name implies, reteaching involves revisiting components of a curriculum with your students. This can serve two purposes:

- helping students better understand concepts they are initially unable to grasp and
- providing additional time for mastery of a concept.

In order to properly reteach students, teachers must first discover what students don't know or understand. This is why relying on the multiple data sources mentioned earlier in this chapter is essential.

Reteaching strategies can include:

- providing real-world examples for students to make a different connection with the information,
- watching videos, and
- peer teaching (sometimes students can learn a concept better from a peer who really understands).

So how would this work in practice? For example, to help students understand the academic vocabulary, one might use as many visuals as possible. Students learn faster and deeper when an image is impressed into their minds. Another strategy could be to simply talk with a student. Ask what he or she understands, and see if the student can verbalize his or her question.

Enrichment

When students demonstrate mastery of a topic, enrichment offers a chance to engage with the information at a higher level, leading to even deeper understanding. Properly executed, enrichment activities can empower students to make the leap from understanding to application. Examples of enrichment strategies can include the following:

- In a reading class, if students demonstrate a mastery of vocabulary, give them a novel to read and focus on high-frequency words.
- In a science class, if students understand your lesson about planets, give them a project that helps them engage. For example, have them write a visitor's guide to a planet of their choice.

Whether you are giving results of an assessment, sharing data, or gathering data, it is crucial to keep parents in the loop. When a student succeeds, the parents can help you encourage the student to keep up the good work. When a student struggles, the parents are armed with the knowledge they need to provide additional assistance at home. In this instance, the more details you can provide the better.

STRATEGIES FOR SUCCESS (WHAT REALLY WORKS)

If you don't take anything else from this chapter, these are the things you need to do to best evaluate and monitor student learning.

Relate Back to Standards

- Standards take the guesswork out of knowing where your students should be with regard to knowledge and understanding.
- Regardless of the type of assessment you utilize, check the data against all applicable standards to make sure your class is on track, preferably exceeding the bar.

Create Hungry Students

- As mentioned before, don't use assessments for gotcha moments. Use them as tools to help make students proud of what they have learned and confident in what they can learn.
- Frame the assessments not as tools for judgment but as tools for empowerment.

Keep Parents Involved

- Data showing that a student is falling behind, excelling, or doing fine (but could be doing better if he or she tried) is just as important and actionable for the parents.
- Making sure parents stay informed of your plans for their children empowers them to help their children succeed.

Teach at a High Level

- Be present, observant, and in the right mindset to gather useful data.
- Be diligent in utilizing the data you collect. Don't squander meaningful information.
- Strive to always provide detailed feedback, which includes all the necessary details and resources students need to improve.

INTERACTIVE EXERCISES

Exercise 1: List the Types of Data You Are Collecting

As mentioned earlier in the chapter, meaningful data is all around you, there for the taking. In this exercise, write down specific examples of data you currently collect every day, week, quarter, and semester.

_____

_____

_____

_____

Exercise 2: List the Ways You Currently Use Data

Now that you have taken stock of the information you currently take in, provide some concrete examples of how you use it to enhance scholastic performance among your students.

_____

_____

_____

_____

Exercise 3: List the Data You *Should* Be Collecting

Now that you've assessed the information you currently gather and what you do with that information, write down some examples of usable data you may be missing.

_____

_____

_____

_____

Exercise 4: List Ways You Could Be Better Using the Data You Collect

In our final exercise, brainstorm ways you could more effectively leverage data. Think in terms of both information you currently collect and information you plan to collect moving forward.

_____
_____
_____
_____

Ultimately, is the data you're gathering useful? Is it complete? Is it actionable? What other observations can you make about the data you collect?

EVALUATION AND SELF-REFLECTION

Developing	I am aware, but I really don't utilize these techniques like I should and I need additional support.
Competent	I am aware, and I occasionally utilize these techniques, however, I am not consistent with implementing these techniques. I may need additional support.
Proficient	I am very skilled in this area, and I utilize these techniques in the classroom with some positive outcomes with students.
Exemplary	I am an expert in this area, and I consistently utilize these techniques in the classroom with significant student results.

Notes:

_____
_____
_____
_____
_____
_____

The following are pertinent questions to ask yourself when assessing your ability to evaluate and monitor student learning. Please rate yourself on the following.

Do you use data to create lessons for your students?			
Developing ☐	Competent ☐	Proficient ☐	Exemplary ☐
Do you provide various forms of assessment? Formative? Summative?			
Developing ☐	Competent ☐	Proficient ☐	Exemplary ☐
Are your learning targets and assessments aligned?			
Developing ☐	Competent ☐	Proficient ☐	Exemplary ☐
Do you provide constant enrichment and remediation based on daily monitoring?			
Developing ☐	Competent ☐	Proficient ☐	Exemplary ☐
Do you quickly provide feedback to students and parents?			
Developing ☐	Competent ☐	Proficient ☐	Exemplary ☐
Do you show students how to assess their own learning?			
Developing ☐	Competent ☐	Proficient ☐	Exemplary ☐

Evaluating & Monitoring Student Learning

Use of Data	Assessment Types	Reteaching/ Enrichment	Parental Notification or Student Progress
Test scores, homework, daily class observations	Formative, Summative, Portfolios, Presentations, Test, Quizzes	Identifying needs for reteaching, remediation, and enrichment	Allow parents to assist in areas of need, inform parents, update system with grades
Developing ☐	Developing ☐	Developing ☐	Developing ☐
Competent ☐	Competent ☐	Competent ☐	Competent ☐
Proficient ☐	Proficient ☐	Proficient ☐	Proficient ☐
Exemplary ☐	Exemplary ☐	Exemplary ☐	Exemplary ☐

Circle of Action: Evaluating and Monitoring Student Learning

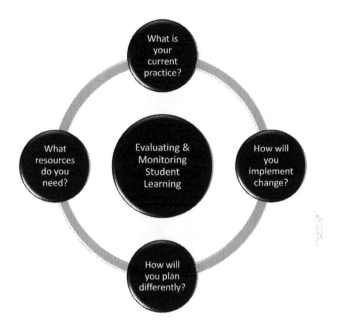

What is your current practice?

_____

_____

_____

How will you implement change?

_____

_____

_____

How will you plan differently?

_____

_____

_____

What resources do you need?

_____

_____

_____

ADDITIONAL RESOURCES

Evaluating and Monitoring Student Learning

- Researchers at Atatürk University examined the positive effects of formative assessment on academic achievement, attitudes toward the lesson, and self-regulation skills. Their study can be found at https://files.eric.ed.gov/fulltext/EJ1179831.pdf.
- A study examining the motivation of student learning using a formative assessment journey can be found at https://www.ncbi.nlm.nih.gov/pmc/articles/PMC3931541/.
- A paper published by the National Council of Teachers of Mathematics that discusses the benefits of formative assessment can be found at https://www.nctm.org/Research-and-Advocacy/Research-Brief-and-Clips/Benefits-of-Formative-Assessment/.

CHAPTER 5
WINNING
The Game Is Professionalism

OVERVIEW

In business, it's commonly suggested that you should dress for the job you want, not the job you have. The saying is so pervasive that the internet is full of memes taking a much-too-literal interpretation of this popular saying. The funniest examples depict people sitting in their cubicles while dressed like astronauts, ninjas, rock stars, or superheroes.

Jokes aside, the spirit of the adage is less about clothing and more about how you prepare for your profession. Thoughtfully speaking, if you are a fitness trainer, you would not show up for a class or session dressed in a business suit.

In other words, what the saying really means is that for people to take you seriously (ideally, seriously enough to give you a raise, promotion, and leadership responsibilities), you need to do more than merely excel in the role you currently occupy. You also need to look, act, and talk in a manner befitting the role you someday wish to play.

In short, to earn the respect of your peers, parents, and, most importantly, students, it is essential to exude professionalism.

What is professionalism? It goes well beyond wearing a suit and tie. In fact, professionalism (or a lack of it) often comes across in subtle and sometimes subconscious ways we tend not to recognize. Unawareness in these crucial areas can harm the careers of otherwise great professionals, which is why I encourage readers to make special notes when they reflect on this chapter.

WHY PROFESSIONALISM IN THE CLASSROOM IS IMPORTANT

Imagine you are a student on the first day of school. Or imagine you are a parent meeting his or her child's teacher for the first time.

What would your first impression be if the teacher walked into the room dressed in sweatpants, with disheveled papers tucked under his or her arm, while talking or texting on a cell phone?

Now imagine a different teacher entering the room in classroom-appropriate attire, with his or her phone silenced and put away and papers neatly arranged in a folder, wearing a friendly yet confident facial expression, focused on the task at hand.

It's possible the first teacher is actually the more talented, experienced, and knowledgeable educator, but which of the two would you be more inclined to take seriously? Which of the two is more likely to earn the respect of his or her students? Which one are you more likely to trust and have confidence in?

Which of these teachers do you resemble more closely? In what ways could you potentially make a more positive impression on your colleagues, parents, and students?

The purpose of this chapter is to examine the many ways you can exude professionalism in your classroom and beyond.

THE MANY FACETS OF PROFESSIONALISM

You may exude professionalism not only through what you wear but also through the way you speak, your mannerisms, the way you conduct yourself in a professional environment, and even a list of intangible qualities that make you a confident and knowledgeable educator.

I am aiming to illustrate here that subliminal cues can be observed (and, in turn, judged) by others in practically limitless ways. But here's the good news: the way you are judged is within your control.

If you strive to exude a higher degree of professionalism, the lowest-hanging fruit is the mastery of basic, obvious cues. A classic example is the practice of housepainters wearing white overalls to subconsciously imply cleanliness.

The challenge, however, is that the human subconscious is powerfully perceptive and nuanced and not easily fooled. For example, how would the perception change if a painter's white overalls were dirty and torn and had huge swaths of spilled paint on them? What would your thoughts be regarding his or her ability to complete the task?

Or how would the perception change if the painter's overalls, boots, ladder, and paint buckets were brand new and didn't have a single smudge on them? You might assume the painter was inexperienced.

To the subconscious, a painter who shows up with well-organized tools and some (but not too many) paint smudges on his or her otherwise clean overalls is going to best instill confidence. In this instance, his or her appearance suggests cleanliness, experience, and, ultimately, professionalism.

As a teacher, it's vital to be aware of these nuances of human perception. Better yet, if you can master subconscious cues, you will have a much easier time earning the respect of students, parents, colleagues, and supervisors. Conversely, failing to do so can undermine even your best-prepared lesson plans.

Following are primary areas to focus your attention on.

BODY LANGUAGE

Have you ever walked into a meeting where the speaker or presenter looked angry? Sad? Nervous? Lacking in confidence? Uninviting? How did that make you feel toward the person? How did it affect how perceptive you were to the speaker's message?

For better or for worse, your body language says a lot. In fact, former FBI agent and noted body-language expert Joe Navarro says that almost 80 percent of communication with others comes from our nonverbal behaviors. Learning how to professionally control our own behaviors and understand those of our students can be a game-changer in the classroom.

In the "Additional Resources" section at the end of this chapter, I will provide a helpful link to a video of a presentation by Mr. Navarro to help you explore body language in depth. But for now, we will review the basics.

Posture

For starters, when you engage with students and colleagues, are your shoulders and back straight? Is your chin up? Or are you slumped over, staring at the floor, holding your arms in an awkward way? Did you realize that your posture speaks about your level of self-esteem and confidence? Indeed it does. If you want to appear effective in your role as an educator, you must project confidence and control in the way you stand, walk, and move about your classroom.

Nonverbal Cues

In addition to good posture, do you refrain from fidgeting? Do you maintain eye contact? Do you offer positive nonverbal cues, such as head nods? Fidgeting and a lack of eye contact can make you seem disinterested, distracted, or nervous. Positive nonverbal cues, on the other hand, communicate that you are engaged with the people around you. These cues show that their thoughts, opinions, and input matter to you.

Mobile Technology

In the age of cell phones, laptops, and tablets, you also must make sure your devices don't become a distraction. Of equal importance, if you are constantly engrossed in your device or phone, you miss out on important information you can gain from the nonverbal cues of people around you. A true professional knows when to close a laptop and provide undivided attention when engaging with others.

Attire

Unless it was Halloween or some other designated fun day, you wouldn't wear a Big Bird costume while teaching, right? If you did, no one would hear anything you said.

Sure, this is an extreme example, but would it be any less distracting to a classroom if you wore inappropriate attire? What about a T-shirt with a divisive political message on it? What about revealing nightclub attire? Torn and dirty jeans? All of these examples serve to illustrate the power attire holds to project an image, whether positive or negative.

As educators, we cannot forget that people (intentionally or not) express themselves through their attire. We can often see the creativity that individuals possess through careful selection of not only clothing but also jewelry, accessories, footwear, hairstyles, and makeup. Conversely, we can infer laziness, a lack of confidence, and other negative traits when a person doesn't pay attention to these variables.

In addition to expressing our individuality, we can also express how we feel through the colors we select. In fact, there is a powerful connection between color and mood. That's why most people wear black to funerals and bright colors when on a beach vacation.

With all of this in mind, ask yourself: What do the clothes you wear say about you? What attire changes could you make in an effort to exemplify a greater level of professionalism?

With such a wide range of variables to consider (clothing, color, footwear, accessories, and so on), it can help to simplify. In my experience as an educator, a good rule of thumb when dressing for the school day is to ask yourself two specific questions:

1. Will this outfit be a potential distraction?
2. Will this outfit positively affect the learning process?

You don't want your clothing to be a distraction; that's self-explanatory. But what does it mean for an outfit to positively affect the learning process?

Positively affecting the learning process means that your clothing should:

- set a tone for education;
- comply with school dress codes;
- provide an appropriate level of formality (be adequately serious without looking too stiff, severe, threatening, or unfriendly); and
- set a positive example for the students to dress for their own success.

Verbal Communication

In chapter 3, we focused on effective communication and building relationships. There is much more to being an effective communicator and professional. Personally and professionally, nonverbal behaviors account for the majority of our communication; however, the manner in which we speak cannot be overlooked. Following are some areas of focus.

Grammar

Young students may not be able to identify poor grammar, but your colleagues and your students' parents most certainly will.

Needless to say, lacking command of the English language will make it more difficult to establish yourself among parents, superiors, and peers as an accomplished educator and an authority on the subjects you teach. Just as important, if you use improper grammar in your classroom, your students will absorb your misuse of language into their own speaking and writing habits.

Foul Language

It should go without saying that swear words have little to no place in a professional environment. In my view, this comes down to risk and reward. There is practically no reward (or value) to using inappropriate language or gossiping at work, but there's plenty of risk in terms of your reputation and standing among parents, students, supervisors, and colleagues. In some instances, foul language could even cost you your job. A true professional will refrain from using less-than-positive language, talking ill of people, or participating in other toxic forms of conversation.

Enunciation and Projection

When speaking, a professional doesn't ramble, veer off topic, or provide unnecessary and distracting details. A professional gets to the point in a clear and concise manner. Imagine if your school leader or superintendent was addressing the school at an event, and you could barely understand what he or she was saying. Maybe the words were mumbled, spoken too quickly to be understood, or spoken too quietly. How would this change your perception of that leader? You expect the principal and other school leaders to speak clearly and with authority. Your students and parents expect the same from you.

Whether you call it slang, idiom, vernacular, or the parlance of our times, using jargon may put you at risk of seeming unprofessional. Sure, it's permissible on occasion to utter an expression that can help you relate to your students. But as a rule, keep your language professional with your students at all times. They will respect you more and appreciate learning from you.

Knowing When to Listen

Finally, when it comes to verbal communication, a true professional knows when it's appropriate to speak and when it's time to listen. Professional communication rarely entails cutting someone off or talking over someone. To the contrary, communicating in a professional manner entails a healthy give-and-take and may even entail inviting people who aren't getting their voices heard to join in on the conversation.

As you examine your verbal communication, put some thought into the nuances of how you speak. Is your speech easy to understand? Do you use proper grammar? Are your words positive and constructive in nature?

Do you effectively engage in constructive two-way conversations with people in your sphere?

Timeliness and Accountability

Have you ever heard the saying "If you're not ten minutes early, you're late"? As we continue to ascend to our highest potential and become the most professional, effective teachers and leaders we can be, it is essential to understand punctuality and accountability.

Obviously, in a day packed full of classes, meetings, and other obligations, it can seem nearly impossible to be early to every meeting. Sometimes it's a struggle simply to be on time. In short, a true professional strives to show up to every meeting, class, or activity on time, prepared, and engaged. A nonprofessional shows up two minutes late, doesn't have notes or lesson plans together, and is not fully present in the activity as it unfolds.

Timeliness and preparation are only half the equation. The other half is accountability.

Another popular saying in the business world is "If you want something done, give it to your busiest person."

Sure, this saying is counterintuitive in that a less busy person would hypothetically have more time and bandwidth to complete your assignment, but the logic is actually sound. Specifically, a person who has proven to be accountable with previous assignments is the best choice to knock out new ones (which is why he or she is so busy in the first place).

Ultimately, a true professional can be trusted and expected to complete the assignment on deadline. A nonprofessional may or may not get it done, which causes a ripple effect among those who count on the completion of this work to execute their own assignments.

When you examine your level of professionalism in the context of timeliness and accountability, how do you rate? Are you someone who shows up on time and is prepared? Are you the one people count on when something important needs to get done? It's a tough question to ask, but it's one that can offer some high-value changes you can make based on your responses.

Your Public Persona

During my first years of teaching in my early twenties, my mother had a habit of scrutinizing my appearance and personal practices. When I would complain about it, she would respond by saying, "You're a teacher now; you can't do certain things. You have to present yourself a certain way at all times, even on weekends and when you're out with your friends."

Twenty years later, I realize she was right! Every time I decided I was going to be free and be me, I would run into my students. Whether I was at the mall, a restaurant, or a theme park, before the adventure was over, I would always hear, "Mrs. Davis! Mrs. Davis!" from a student who invariably had his or her parents in tow. The students would always be excited to see me and tell all their friends. It was a mini–celebrity moment, and I wanted to make sure I was providing a healthy example for them. I'll come right out and say it: it's not fair.

Most people get to go to work; then go out with their friends, do and say what they want, and post pictures and opinions on social media; and then show up to their jobs the next day. As teachers, we don't have that luxury. Like it or not, professional educators are public figures and role models, just like politicians, athletes, and celebrities. As such, we must be cognizant of the optics of our personal lives.

Because we deal directly with students and parents, we have to consider our off-the-clock behavior and the perception it will create. To put a finer point on it:

- We are asking the community to trust us with their children.
- It is our job to set a positive example for our students.

While this represents a sizable responsibility, we must embrace our status as role models and conduct ourselves in a manner worthy of the public's trust at all times. That's what you signed up for, so always be conscious of the example you're setting in everything you do.

Fortunately, this doesn't take away your creativity and personal life. You can still be you. It just means the version of you the public sees commands respect in your expertise while helping your students become everything they can be.

As a mentor of mine used to say, "Don't get creative with the rules. Get creative with the instruction."

As you consider your own behavior, think about how you dress and act when in public. Perhaps more importantly, ask yourself what your Facebook or Instagram page says about you. What about Snap? Twitter? Pinterest? It all matters.

Professionalism in a Modern Digital World

After reading this chapter, you may be thinking to yourself that old-school definitions of professionalism have faded over time. For example, places of work have become a lot more casual and less strict and formal. In turn, traditional barometers of professionalism (e.g., a suit and tie, a firm handshake, an expensive briefcase, a formal style of speech, and so on) are somewhat less relevant today. In some respects, you're right.

In addition to less formality, mobile technology, the pandemic, and other scenarios have forced workplace etiquette to evolve and continue to evolve as we tend to do more on our smartphones and devices than we do in person.

Think about the workplace today versus the workplace of ten or even five years ago. When we look at what was acceptable then versus now, we see that things are much different. We have gone from times when ladies were advised to wear only knee-length skirts to a time when you can basically conduct a business meeting in your pajamas from your living room with Skype or Zoom.

But before you donate your dress clothes and stock up on lounge clothes and fuzzy socks, consider the following: as educators, we do our most important work in face-to-face situations. Because of the in-person nature of our jobs, we must not forget the importance of nurturing relationships, growth, and behaviors.

How do we accomplish this? By embracing long-standing definitions of professionalism that still apply in modern society and combining them with an ability to navigate the pitfalls of professionalism in a digital age.

MODELING BEHAVIOR (SERVING AS AN EXAMPLE OF PROFESSIONALISM)

Thus far in the chapter, I have talked about professionalism in more general terms, offering some examples here and there.

If you're serious about exuding professionalism in your work and personal life, now is a good time to outline some additional low-hanging fruit.

Here's a list of concrete, easy-to-implement changes you can make that will immediately help position you as a professional and serve as a positive example to others:

- Be on time to work and meetings.
- Complete tasks on or before the deadline.
- Volunteer for additional responsibilities, such as bus or lunch duty.
- Proactively make parent contacts.
- Submit and share lesson plans or creative ideas with teammates.
- Follow the code of conduct and school rules.
- Go through the proper channels to make positive changes to school rules (e.g., submitting ideas at school board meetings or making constructive suggestions to your supervisors).

EVALUATION AND SELF-REFLECTION

Developing	I am aware, but I really don't utilize these techniques like I should and I need additional support.
Competent	I am aware, and I occasionally utilize these techniques, however, I am not consistent with implementing these techniques. I may need additional support.
Proficient	I am very skilled in this area, and I utilize these techniques in the classroom with some positive outcomes with students.
Exemplary	I am an expert in this area, and I consistently utilize these techniques in the classroom with significant student results.

Notes:

_____

_____

_____

_____

_____

_____

_____

_____

_____

_____

_____

_____

_____

_____

_____

_____

_____

_____

_____

_____

_____

_____

The following are pertinent questions to ask yourself when evaluating and monitoring your level of professionalism. Please rate yourself on the following.

How do you start each day? Do you have a plan or routine you follow?			
Developing ☐	Competent ☐	Proficient ☐	Exemplary ☐
Do you walk into your classroom daily with a smile or a scowl?			
Developing ☐	Competent ☐	Proficient ☐	Exemplary ☐
Do you always speak professionally to students, colleagues, and parents?			
Developing ☐	Competent ☐	Proficient ☐	Exemplary ☐
Do you exhibit positive body language?			
Developing ☐	Competent ☐	Proficient ☐	Exemplary ☐
Are you welcoming and inviting to students and parents?			
Developing ☐	Competent ☐	Proficient ☐	Exemplary ☐
Is your attire professional daily?			
Developing ☐	Competent ☐	Proficient ☐	Exemplary ☐
Do you submit lesson plans and other requests in a timely manner?			
Developing ☐	Competent ☐	Proficient ☐	Exemplary ☐
Do you manage personal and professional time wisely?			
Developing ☐	Competent ☐	Proficient ☐	Exemplary ☐
Do you ever think about your body language? What are some intentional nonverbal actions you take to create a professional or effective environment? Provide some examples here.			

Let's be honest: we all have moments when we drop below professional standards. This chapter is intended to help you create habits that transfer into developing the professional you desire to be.

Professionalism

Body Language	Attire	Communication	Meeting Deadlines
Facial expressions, hand gestures, tone, attitude towards teaching	Business professional, casual, spirit days	Written, verbal, tone	Lesson plans, IEPs, Emails, Phone Calls, Feedbacks
Developing ☐	Developing ☐	Developing ☐	Developing ☐
Competent ☐	Competent ☐	Competent ☐	Competent ☐
Proficient ☐	Proficient ☐	Proficient ☐	Proficient ☐
Exemplary ☐	Exemplary ☐	Exemplary ☐	Exemplary ☐

Circle of Action: Evaluating and Monitoring Professionalism

What is your current practice?

_____

_____

_____

How will you implement change?

_____

_____

_____

How will you plan differently?

_____

_____

_____

What resources do you need?

_____

_____

_____

ADDITIONAL RESOURCES

Professionalism

- Video of former FBI agent and current body-language expert Joe Navarro gives a presentation of the power of nonverbal communication. Visit https://www.youtube.com/watch?v=HRl0dvPRkSI to watch.
- Business Insider offers eleven examples of common body-language mistakes and offers insights on how to correct them. Visit https://www.businessinsider.com/common-body-language-mistakes-employees-make-2014-4 to learn more.
- The following blog article on the website of the Outliers book series offers useful insights into creating a culture of learning in the classroom: http://www.ingredientsofoutliers.com/7-powerful-tips-for-creating-a-culture-of-learning-in-the-classroom/.

CHAPTER 6
MEASURING YOUR SUCCESS
Goals—Let's Go!

OVERVIEW

As they say, knowledge is power. At this point in the book, you should be armed with a significant amount of new knowledge in the form of strategies, insights, and self-reflection.

But even the most powerful knowledge can be ineffective in the absence of execution. In other words, now that you know what to do, it's time to do it!

Before we get ahead of ourselves, however, we need a strategic, intelligently conceived plan in place. As this chapter's title ("Measuring Your Success: Goals—Let's Go!") suggests, the purpose of this part of the book is to define a framework for setting goals and affecting positive change in your classroom.

To get things started, let's talk a bit about change and how to manage it.

MANAGING CHANGE

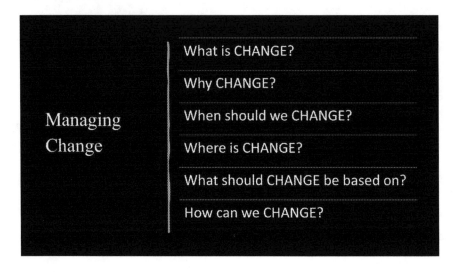

For practically anyone (myself included), change can be scary and uncomfortable.

To help get over the initial feeling of fear and dread, I have found it helpful to psyche myself up for change with some inspirational quotes. To kick this chapter off, here are some of my favorites:

"The greatest discovery of all time is that a person can
change his future by merely changing his attitude."
—Oprah Winfrey

"Everyone thinks of changing the world, but
no one thinks of changing himself."
—Leo Tolstoy

"Play to your strengths. If you aren't great at
something, do more of what you're great at."
—Jason Lemkin

Now that we're in the right frame of mind, let's get to work!

What Is Change?

Depending on the context, change can mean many different things. Change is the act of putting different clothes on, the money a cashier gives you when you pay for something in cash, the act of transferring between two buses or trains, and so on. But the change I am referring to here pertains to the direction you have pointed your classroom and the path you and your students are currently traveling. Specifically, if you are not on a path to meet an educational objective in your classroom, you have to change course. Depending on the situation, change may require only a slight correction, or you might need to travel in a different direction entirely.

To put it another way, when thinking about change, imagine yourself as the captain of a ship. Your students are your crew. The shoreline beyond the horizon is your goal. Change is the force that, no matter which way the wind starts blowing or what storm might be brewing, empowers you to keep moving toward and eventually reach your goal.

Why Should We Change?

Our environment is constantly changing. If we remain static, what might work for us today could be irrelevant and useless tomorrow.

Consider technology. Prior to 2007, when the iPhone was released, everyone was using flip phones, and the Motorola RAZR was the world's most popular model. But once people made the jump to smartphones, naturally, people stopped buying flip phones.

Motorola, not quick enough to change their focus to smartphones, went from the number-one phone maker to an also-ran. If you think about it, Motorola was going to undergo a change no matter what. But instead of proactively being the agent of change, they allowed the change to happen to them, and it happened practically overnight and certainly wasn't the change they wanted.

This is an extreme example, but it illustrates how the ability to survive can be dependent on the capacity for change. Do you want to be the force of change in your teaching career, or do you want change forced upon you?

When Should We Change?

We should be changing constantly.

I'm not necessarily talking about a pop-diva-esque reinvention of yourself. But you should be constantly learning, growing, and considering new perspectives. You should also be adapting your teaching style to accommodate shifts in educational standards, the way students learn, current teaching techniques, and best practices.

These efforts are often referred to as *continuous-improvement initiatives.* In fact, corporations of all sizes invest heavily in programs, such as LEAN and Kaizen, to help stay competitive.

To stay competitive in your classroom, school, and district, you should maintain a rate of change that, at the very least, keeps you current and, ideally, puts you ahead of the trends.

Where Is Change?

As a teacher, most of the changes you can make will naturally take place within the confines of your school building. Obvious examples include decluttering your classroom to remove visual distractions, rearranging the desks to improve attention and focus, and planning your lessons in ways that keep students engaged. But teaching-related changes don't necessarily have to take place in the classroom. For example, if you are struggling to be ready by the time your students show up each morning, you may need some changes at home. Changes could include picking out your clothes before you go to bed, getting to sleep on time, setting an earlier alarm, reviewing your lesson plans while you eat breakfast in your kitchen, and making time to stay informed on new teaching methods and trends.

It's also important to consider that changes don't necessarily have to be tangible and physical or take place in the outside world. An effective change could include altering your mindset, emotions, or feelings. You could make the choice not to be bothered by a gossipy coworker. Or you could choose to be grateful for the daily opportunity to shape young minds, instead of choosing to view teaching as simply a job you have to go to. You could also decide to listen more when talking to people who have opinions different from yours, to try to better understand their points of view.

Ultimately, a change that positively affects your teaching or your life can take place in your mind, in your classroom, in your home, and beyond. In other words, if the change makes you a more effective person, the change should take place wherever it can.

Change Based on Data

As I will touch on here and then expand on later in this chapter, effective change is data-driven. Would professional basketball players be better served by gauging improvement on how they feel they are playing or by monitoring stats, such as free throw percentage and rebounds per game, not to mention the team's win-loss record?

The same holds true in your classroom. You might feel you have made changes that improve your instruction, but if you don't have metrics to back it up, your feelings may be unreliable. The majority of changes you make in your classroom should be based on meaningful, measurable data that quantifies positive impact on your class.

Measure yourself by creating benchmarks for your students and monitoring their progress. If your change initiative increases comprehension, test performance, engagement, participation, enthusiasm, or preparation for future coursework, then the change was effective and necessary. If it doesn't, then reexamine the change and the data, and make adjustments to meet the need.

For example, imagine for a moment that you are a world-class athlete training for an upcoming competition. You create a [lesson] plan that includes fitness, technique, strategy, mental toughness, and nutrition. During the course of training, everything seems to be working, with the exception of your weight goal. If you set a goal to either gain or lose a certain amount of weight by a certain date before the event and your daily monitor (the scale) is not moving in the right direction, you can make a necessary adjustment to get the results you want. You may add more protein to your diet, or you may decrease the carbs. Either way, you make a change based on the data and progress.

The same concept applies with regard to our students and instructional delivery. We need to set goals, monitor progress, and make adjustments along the way to get the results we want.

Change Based on Relevance to Your Goals

Whether in your personal life or in your professional life, change should support your goals.

Consider someone who has a goal to achieve a better work-life balance. Then consider someone who wants a big promotion.

Since these are vastly different goals, the types of required change(s) to support these goals would also need to be different.

The person who wants a better work-life balance might target a role within his or her organization that offers less responsibility, a more flexible schedule, and shorter hours. The obvious trade-off will be lower pay and fewer opportunities for advancement.

In contrast, the person who wants the big promotion will commit to various sacrifices, such as longer hours, continuing education, and potential travel. The trade-off will be less time to spend with family and friends, as well as an increase in responsibility, pressure, and possibly stress.

With regard to teaching, change should support:

- your goals as an educator (for example, do you eventually want to become a department head or an administrator?);
- your personal happiness and well-being (you can't be effective at your job if you're unhappy); and
- the collective goals of your students.

How Do We Change?

In their book *Implementing Change: Patterns, Principles, and Potholes*, authors Gene E. Hall and Shirley M. Hord outline in depth their principles of change. If you're looking for maximum success when affecting change in your classroom, their concepts and findings are well worth a read. Here are some quick highlights to consider:

- Change is a process, not an event.
- There are significant differences in what is entailed in the development and implementation of an innovation.
- An organization does not change until individuals within it change.
- Interventions are the actions and events that are key to the success of the change process.
- There will be no change in outcomes until new practices are implemented.
- Administrative leadership is essential to change success.
- Facilitating change is a team process.
- Appropriate interventions reduce change resistance.

Another concept I've found helpful is Kurt Lewin's change theory.

Imagine you have a large cube of ice, but you realize you want the ice to be shaped like a cone. What do you do?

Since the ice is frozen, you can't simply shape it into a cone; it will break.

First, you must make the ice amenable to change—in other words, you must melt it into water. Once the ice is melted into a changeable form, you can mold it. Finally, once the water is formed into the shape you want, you can refreeze it to make the shape permanent.

Lewin's analogy makes sense because it accurately represents the process of how people change. Specifically, his process of unfreezing, changing, and refreezing requires prior learning and ideas to be reevaluated; modified where necessary; and, finally, solidified.

As you utilize the reflections made throughout the book, think in these terms:

1. The unfreezing entails honest reflection of your current ideas and processes. Use some form of data to validate the thoughts and reflections. Change needs to happen based on real data, not emotion.
2. The change entails adopting new ideas and processes while moving away from the old ones.
3. Finally, refreezing represents the creation and execution of new plans, initiatives, and programs.

Affecting Change within Ourselves

As we melt (reflect), let's create some plans to unfreeze, change, and refreeze our classrooms into new shapes.

Based on your reflections, list your top five priorities for change. (Note: I recommend one priority from each chapter.)

1.
2.
3.
4.
5.

Now that you know what needs to change, let's set some goals!

DEVELOPING SMART GOALS

Hopefully, as you set goals for your classroom, your overarching objective as a teacher is to maximize student success through effective instruction. For that to happen, not just any goals will do. Your goals need to be SMART.

What are SMART goals? Read on to find out.

SMART is an acronym for the five criteria your goals must meet in order to be worthwhile. In other words, if a goal doesn't stack up in these five areas, the goal needs to be revised, expanded upon, or replaced with something more workable:

S **Specific**
M **Measurable**
A **Attainable**
R **Realistic (or Relevant)**
T **Timely**

To get the ball rolling, we will start with an example of a vague (not-SMART) goal, followed by examples that are SMART.

- <u>Not</u> SMART
  - o "My goal is to see my students improve."

- SMART
  - o "My goal is to see my students increase homework completion by 5 percent over the following two-week period. I plan to achieve this goal by actively tracking homework completion, identifying students who aren't completing homework, and proactively working with the students and their parents to incentivize good homework habits."
  - o "My goal is to identify specific areas of difficulty with each student in my class and adjust my teaching accordingly. I plan to achieve this goal over the next six weeks by allocating five minutes per week of one-on-one time with each of my students. I also will measure my progress by tracking the amount of time I spend with each student and correlating that with improvements in test scores."
  - o "My goal is to make sure every student is actively contributing to lab activities, so the most enthusiastic ones don't excel while the others fall behind. I plan to achieve this goal by the end of the quarter, track the participation of each student, and correlate increased participation with test scores at the end of the semester."

Now that you have some examples, let's break down the five criteria.

Specific

As a teacher, it's certainly noble to say, "My goal is to be a better teacher." But if you actually intend to foster self-improvement, your goals must be less vague. To make your goals worthwhile, pinpoint a well-defined area of focus, and then fill in the who, what, where, when, how, and why.

Using the activities sample goal from above, let's fill in the blanks.

- Who is involved in the goal?
  - o Students taking my chemistry course.

- What am I trying to accomplish?
  o An increase in active participation in hands-on lab activities.
- Where is this taking place?
  o In the school science lab.
- When am I starting, and when do I plan to achieve the goal?
  o I will start immediately and plan to achieve 100 percent participation by the end of the quarter.
- How am I going to achieve the goal?
  o I will observe and track participation, identify students who aren't participating adequately, and then step in to take measures to get them more involved.
- Why am I doing this?
  o Students gain a better understanding (and, in turn, perform better on tests) when they participate in hands-on activities.

When setting your own goals, answer these questions to ensure they are adequately specific.

Measurable

Another crucial aspect of goal setting is applying metrics to them. These are things you can measure and quantify.

With reference to the examples outlined above, a goal such as "Seeing my students improve" is hard to attach numbers to.

A proper goal, conversely, will be easy to evaluate. For example:

- How did they improve?
  o Improved test scores
- How much did they improve?
  o 10 percent
- How quickly did they improve?
  o 1 percent per week over a ten-week time period

When setting your goal-based initiatives, make sure they can be measured.

Attainable

If your high school's football team went 1–9 last season, mandating that the coaches shoot for a state championship this season isn't really reasonable.

An attainable goal will require a healthy amount of dedication, discipline, and effort, but it should also be within reach.

In other words, the coaching staff would be better served by a well-conceived plan for steady incremental improvement over several years. Perhaps they strive to win three games this season. The following season, they aim for a winning record.

By the team's setting and meeting a series of attainable goals, the chance of eventually winning a state championship (or at least winning the conference) is not as far-fetched.

Using this logic, don't set out to be Teacher of the Year if you currently preside over an underperforming class.

Instead, set a series of smaller, more attainable goals over the next several weeks, quarters, and school years. Over time, your students could be among the highest-performing in the district, and that prestigious teaching award could be within your grasp.

Realistic (or Relevant)

The words *attainable* and *realistic* may seem similar and can easily be confused with each other. In truth, they mean very different things.

In fact, a goal can be attainable but unrealistic at the same time. Here's an example.

Assuming you're in good health and really want to, you could complete an Ironman triathlon. Many people have done it, and with dedication and discipline, it's an attainable goal for you too.

But is it realistic? You need to ask yourself if the goal is relevant to other goals and priorities in your life. Let's examine:

- Ironman training requires countless long hours of training.
- Equipment and coaching can be expensive.
- Your dietary requirements change dramatically.

- Participating in the event typically entails travel and complex logistics, including shipping your bike, wetsuit, and other gear.
- The time and monetary commitments of training and competing require you to make sacrifices in other areas of your life.
  - o Do you want to take a college course? Forget it.
  - o Do you want to go on a beach vacation with the family? No way.
  - o Do you want to have dinner and drinks with your friends? Nope.
  - o Do you want to save for a down payment on a house? Tough to do when you also need to buy a carbon-fiber triathlon bike and hire a coach.

The same holds true with classroom goals. It may be possible for your class to read *War and Peace* this semester, but if you need your students to collectively improve their standardized test scores in science, that might not be realistic.

In short, each goal needs to be consistent with your other goals while fitting in with your long-term objectives.

Timely

Referring back to the section about specific goals, you may have noticed that each SMART goal had a well-defined timeline attached. These timelines include start dates (either specified or implied) and target dates.

Why? Without deadlines, there is no sense of urgency. It's also more difficult to develop a timeline from which you can create tasks and milestones.

Creating Your SMART Goals

Now, based on the top five priorities for change, it's time to create your SMART goals.

Goal 1 _____

Goal 2 _____

Goal 3 _____

Goal 4 _____

Goal 5 _____

Action!

What actions will you take to achieve these goals? Commit to the action plan for success.

Action Plan

Priority	SMART Goal	Action Steps	Timeline	Outcome
EXAMPLE Classroom Management	Decrease the number of classroom referrals by 10 percent in the next four weeks	Call parents and set up conferences and contracts for students with discipline concerns	• Call all parents by next Friday • Create a student contract by Monday	
Classroom Organization and Management				
Instructional Planning and Delivery				
Effective Communication and Positive Relationships				
Evaluating and Monitoring Student Learning				
Professionalism				

CONCLUSION

As I wrote the final chapters of this book, my family and I were hunkered down in our home, observing social distancing and sheltering-in-place requirements necessitated by the COVID-19 outbreak.

If you were teaching during this time, you experienced an unprecedented degree of change. Specifically, you had to end the school year by abruptly (and without warning) shifting to a 100 percent distance-learning program. Most likely, you had never executed a distance-learning program, and your school's IT department probably had all of two weeks to create the digital infrastructure to support it. The curriculum changed, technology changed, and interaction with your students changed. Everything was suddenly different. You had to simultaneously learn and teach. You were coming to grips with the notion that for the foreseeable future (and possibly forever), teaching would never be the same.

With regard to the exercise in the introduction of this book, our desert islands got a lot bigger and quite a bit lonelier, and the toolboxes we relied on for years were stuck on faraway shores. It was time to sink or swim, and we got to see what we were made of.

In the COVID-19 quarantine era, were you a proactive agent of positive change (like the iPhone), or did the change make you less relevant and effective (like the RAZR)? In other words, how did you adapt? What changes did you make for yourself, for your students and other stakeholders?

Using the principles outlined in this book, let's examine.

Classroom Organization and Management

- Did you reconfigure your classroom (both the real one and the virtual one) for effective teaching while still meeting social-distancing requirements?
- Did you do your best to equip your students with the e-learning tools and knowledge they needed to succeed?
- Did you make the transition(s) between classroom-based instruction and e-learning seamless for your students?

Instructional Planning and Delivery

- How did you give instruction differently to accommodate distance learning?
- Did you leverage technology or let it become a barrier?
- Did you adapt your lesson plans to address the changes in the way students learned differently (e.g., schedules and daily routines)?

Effective Communication and Positive Relationships

- How did you interact with your stakeholders?
- How did you ensure that you effectively communicated and delivered to students and parents?
- Were you a source of emotional support to your students and parents (who collectively were experiencing stressful and disruptive situations of their own)?

Evaluating and Monitoring Student Learning

- Did you devise new ways to collect, measure, and assess data?
- Based on the data, were you able to uphold your previous levels of teaching effectiveness?

Professionalism

- Did you take your personal and professional self to the next level?
- Did you uphold a professional demeanor despite the pitfalls of working from home (such as children, pets, spouses, and distractions)?

Measuring Your Success

- Did you develop SMART goals to maximize the effectiveness of your instruction in these new education paradigms?

  o Specific?
  o Measurable?
  o Attainable?
  o Realistic?
  o Timely?

No matter how you answer these questions and no matter how you feel you did, I'm here to tell you that you are a hero. Simply by putting aside your own set of fears and stepping far out of your comfort zone, you performed an amazing service to your students. For that, I'm grateful, and your community is grateful.

As we close out this book, however, it's now time to look to the future. Here are some parting thoughts:

- The strategies outlined in this book are guaranteed to improve your professional and personal self, no matter what the education environment throws at you. Internalize them, and execute them faithfully.

- I can't stress enough the need for data to affect positive change that is measurable and meaningful. As they say, knowledge is power.
- When future challenges come up, remember how we move forward:

    o Data
    o Plan
    o Action
    o Reflection

Connect with me @onyourmark_getsetgoal, and let me know how it's going!

Printed in the United States
by Baker & Taylor Publisher Services